GETTYSBURG

To Roy Heidecker

Warm Regards from

Jim McPherson

For Roy Heidicker
From Sea to shining USC!
All the best —
Ron Maxwell
June 20 '94

©MKünstler '92

THE PAINTINGS OF MORT KÜNSTLER

GETTYSBURG

TEXT BY JAMES M. McPHERSON

Turner Publishing, Inc.

ATLANTA

For Deborah

Published by Turner Publishing, Inc.
A Subsidiary of Turner Broadcasting System, Inc.
1050 Techwood Drive, N.W.
Atlanta, Georgia 30318

First Edition 10 9 8 7 6 5 4 3 2
Hardcover: ISBN 1-878685-79-1
Library of Congress Catalog Card Number: 93-60663

Distributed by Andrews and McMeel
A Universal Press Syndicate Company
4900 Main Street
Kansas City, Missouri 64112

EDITORIAL:

ALAN SCHWARTZ, EDITOR
KATHERINE BUTTLER, ASSOCIATE EDITOR
CRAWFORD BARNETT, EDITORIAL ASSISTANT

DESIGN:

MICHAEL J. WALSH, DESIGN DIRECTOR
KAREN E. SMITH, BOOK AND COVER DESIGN, PRODUCTION
MARTY MOORE, PHOTO RESEARCH
ANNE MURDOCH, PRODUCTION COORDINATOR
KEVIN D. SMITH, TITLE DESIGN

COLOR SEPARATIONS AND FILM PREPARATION BY HI-TECH COLOR, SMYRNA, GEORGIA.
PRINTING BY INLAND PRESS, MENOMONEE FALLS, WISCONSIN.

PRINTED IN THE U.S.A.

Table of Contents

Foreword

There are probably more people in these United States who know the opening lines of Lincoln's Gettysburg Address than there are citizens aware of the details of that momentous battle, the turning point of the Civil War.

And I was one of them, until I had the opportunity to play the role of Robert E. Lee in the TNT epic film *Gettysburg*, adapted from Michael Shaara's Pulitzer Prize–winning novel, *The Killer Angels*. Then I began to study the man and the period in earnest, to learn what I could to enhance my interpretation of Lee, an enigmatic Virginian who favored neither secession nor slavery, but whose sense of honor demanded that allegiance to his native state supersede loyalty to the nation.

If we look at this horrific conflict in the conventional retelling, the truisms of Northern industrialism attempting to impose an egalitarian ideal upon Southern agrarianism, of plantation feudalism protecting its privilege, of the test whether or not a voluntary political marriage of states could end in divorce—all these apply.

But *Gettysburg* leaves those questions to the history books: right and wrong, good and evil, are not the concern here, nor are the political distinctions. The focus is on the people who faced each other on the battlefield for three long days of brutal combat in July 1863. From generals to infantry volunteers, the human beings who fought loyally and valiantly for Union or Confederacy—this is their story. How the great battle that consumed thousands of American lives was won, and lost, because of chance, and the skill or ineptitude of men, not causes. *Gettysburg* is the human story behind the great battle.

To stand on the "hallowed ground" of the Gettysburg battlefield and imagine the horror and the glory is in itself a spiritual experience. To live the experience as an actor in the epic and recreate it for a film audience is an honor, and I am proud to have been part of the reenactment that will make our history come to life for millions of viewers.

The companion book, *Gettysburg*, also brings the battle to life. Accurately and compassionately painted by noted artist Mort Künstler and forcefully narrated by Pulitzer Prize–winning historian James McPherson, this book is a permanent and accurate record of the fighters in their battle regalia, precisely rendered and flawlessly executed: a story of human motives and triumphs and defeats with words and pictures so carefully integrated that the book is destined to become a classic.

It is powerful stuff, and I can only hope that it will prove to be as momentous an experience for the viewer and reader as it was for me and an extraordinary army of fellow players.

Martin Sheen

The Artist's Acknowledgments

I went to Gettysburg for the first time in March 1988. It was to do research for a painting that would later become the "High Water Mark." This became a turning point in my career. I was so inspired by the visit that I have returned again and again—more times than I can count. John Earnst, the Superintendent of the National Military Park at the time, was friendly and cooperative, as was the entire staff. Kathy Harrison, the Chief Historian, then and now, helped in every way to make the work as accurate as possible, and the painting was later unveiled by New York senator Al D'Amato at the park museum on the 125th anniversary of the battle.

On that first visit to Gettysburg, I met Ted Sutphen of American Print Gallery, who published the "High Water Mark" as a limited edition print. Many more prints have followed. I thank him for sharing his knowledge, his counseling, and his advice in the preparation of this book, and for his friendship.

I thank Professor James McPherson for honoring me with his fascinating and informative text. I hope there will be future collaborations.

I am indebted to the present Superintendent of the Park, José Cisneros, for giving me the honor of displaying my Civil War paintings in 1992 and the paintings from this book during the 1993 season.

My gratitude to Richard Lynch, Director of The Hammer Galleries in New York City, for bringing my work to the attention of the art world and for exhibiting this collection of Gettysburg paintings in November 1993.

My appreciation to my good friend, historian-writer Rod Gragg, for providing the impetus to get this project under way.

The accuracy I have achieved could not have been possible without the constant advice of John Heiser and the countless other historians who have been so free in sharing their expertise.

I enjoyed working with book designer Karen Smith. This beautiful book is the result of her creativity and dedication.

My daughter, Jane, and Paula McEvoy have been invaluable in all of the everyday tasks of a busy studio. I cannot thank them enough for their patience and understanding.

And my heartfelt and sincerest appreciation and love to my dear Deborah for helping in every conceivable way to complete this book, the most difficult project of my career.

Mort Künstler

THE ROADS TO GETTYSBURG

P A R T · O N E

In the spring of 1863 the American Civil War entered its third year. The conflict had already cost the lives of 150,000 Union and 100,000 Confederate soldiers. The naive optimism of both sides in 1861—that the war would last only a few months—had long since disappeared. It had been replaced by war weariness and divisions within both the Union and Confederacy over the strategy and purpose of the war. The administrations of Abraham Lincoln and Jefferson Davis were determined to prevail no matter what the cost.

★ ★

AFTER A YEAR OF REMARKABLE VICTORIES, THE FAME OF ROBERT E. LEE HAD SPREAD THROUGH THE ENGLISH-SPEAKING WORLD. IN THE NORTH, EVEN PATRIOTIC UNIONISTS ADMIRED LEE AND LONGED FOR A GENERAL OF EQUAL ABILITY TO COMMAND THE ARMY OF THE POTOMAC. AS LEE RODE NORTHWARD NEAR HAGERSTOWN ON JUNE 26, 1863, HEADING TOWARD A FATEFUL APPOINTMENT AT GETTYS-BURG, A MARYLAND WOMAN ON THE ROADSIDE HOLDING AN AMERICAN FLAG WAS HEARD TO SAY: "OH, I WISH HE WAS OURS."

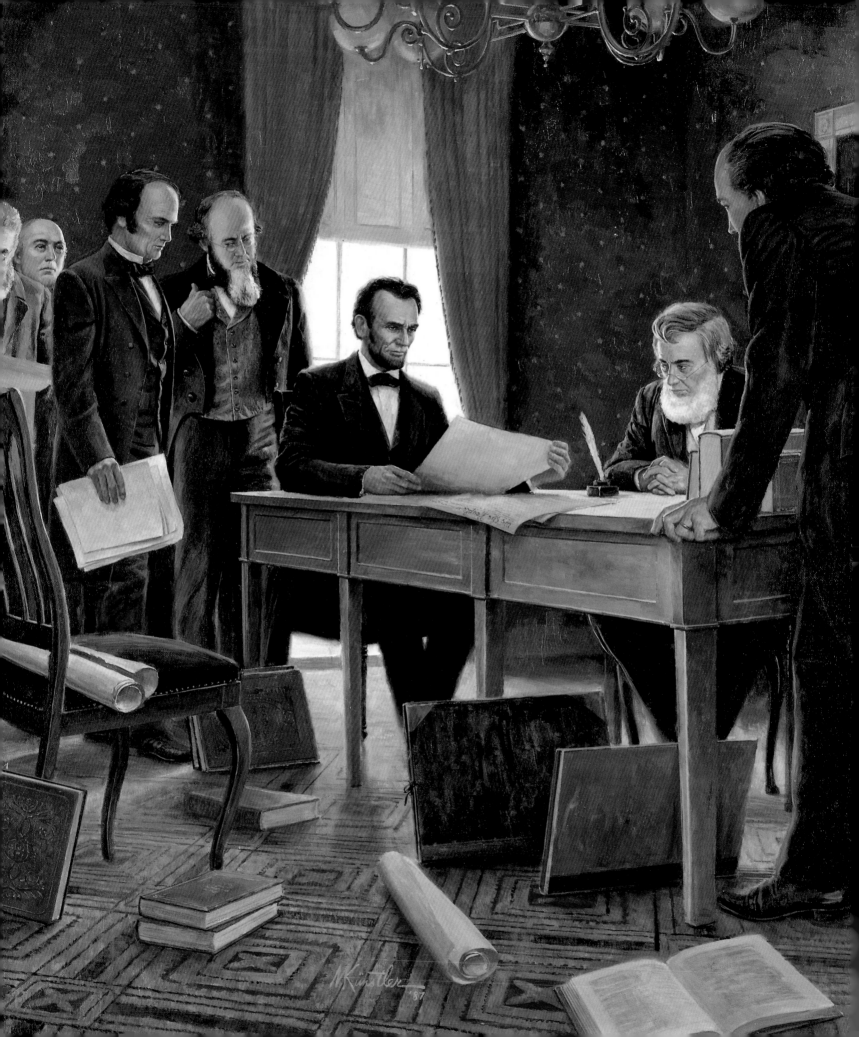

Most soldiers on both sides felt the same way. They were volunteers who had enlisted with a firm resolve to preserve the United States as one nation indivisible or to achieve independence for the new Confederate States of America.

The Confederate government had been forced to enact conscription in April 1862 to fill up the ranks. The Union government had compelled a militia draft in some states in the summer of 1862 and had passed a national conscription law in March 1863. In most cases, the draftees and substitutes did not share the determination and high morale of the volunteers. And the letters home from many soldiers, volunteers and draftees alike, expressed homesickness and a longing for peace. Their families dreaded the coming of spring 1863 with its renewed military campaigns and lengthened casualty lists. A new song appeared that year to express these sentiments, "When This Cruel War Is Over." Its haunting melody and poignant lyrics made it popular immediately in both North and South, and more than a million copies of sheet music were sold.

> Weeping, sad and lonely,
> Hopes and fears how vain!
> When this cruel war is over,
> Praying that we meet again.

But no one in the spring of 1863 could predict with confidence when the war would be over. For Abraham Lincoln, the end would come when Confederate armies surrendered or dispersed and Southern states returned to the Union. Jefferson Davis was determined to fight until Union armies withdrew from Confederate territory and the United States recognized Confederate independence. These conflicting aims were uncompromisable. Yet opposition factions from both the North and South—especially the Northern Peace Democrats, or "Copperheads" —demanded compromise. They urged an armistice and negotiations to end the slaughter. Lincoln made compromise even more difficult with his Emancipation Proclamation, issued on January 1, 1863. The

Lincoln administration now insisted on freedom and Union as conditions of peace; the South stood to lose slavery as well as independence if it yielded. Peace looked further off than ever.

In both North and South the antiwar factions grew more vociferous when the war went badly for their side. By the spring of 1863 the North was taking heavy losses. During the previous year, however, the course of the conflict and the resultant morale, both Northern and Southern, had zigzagged like a seismograph during an earthquake. A dazzling series of Union naval and military victories during the first five months of 1862 had given Northern forces control of Kentucky, most of Tennessee, the Mississippi River except for Vicksburg, and much of the South Atlantic coast. Many of the Confederacy's most important cities had fallen, among them New Orleans, Baton Rouge, Memphis, Nashville, and Norfolk.

Jefferson Davis's inauguration as president of the Confederacy occurred on February 22, 1862 (until then he had been provisional president), a few days after the loss of Forts Henry and Donelson in Tennessee and Roanoke Island in North Carolina. Davis and his Negro footmen in the inaugural procession wore black suits. When asked why, the coachman replied dryly: "This, ma'am, is the way we always does in Richmond at funerals and sichlike."

Three months later, Richmond itself seemed doomed to capture as George B. McClellan's powerful Army of the Potomac advanced to within five miles of the Confederate capital. Jefferson Davis's government packed its archives and treasury on trains for evacuation. "The cause of the Union now marches on in every section of the country," exulted the North's leading newspaper, the *New York Tribune*, in May 1862. "Every blow tells fearfully against the rebellion. The rebels themselves are panic-stricken, or despondent. It now requires no very far-reaching prophet to predict the end of the struggle."

But the *Tribune* proved to be a poor prophet. Like

a battered but game boxer, the Confederacy picked itself up and counterpunched so fiercely that within four months it had knocked Union forces back on the ropes. The South's eccentric, secretive genius, Stonewall Jackson, and the audacious, astute Robert E. Lee master-minded these counteroffensives.

With a small, highly mobile army, Jackson won several victories over larger Union forces in Virginia's Shenandoah Valley during May and June 1862, compelling Lincoln to withhold reinforcements from McClellan's campaign against Richmond. On June 1, Lee took command of what he renamed the Army of Northern Virginia when its previous commander, Joseph E. Johnston, was wounded in the battle of Seven Pines, an unsuccessful effort to drive back McClellan's advancing army. Lee dispatched his dashing cavalry leader, Jeb Stuart, on a reconnaissance to locate the best point for an attack on McClellan. Stuart not only discovered that the Union right flank was vulnerable; he also made a complete circuit around the Army of the Potomac, destroying supplies and returning to his own base without significant loss, a spectacular exploit that catapulted Stuart to fame.

Lee brought Jackson from the Shenandoah Valley to Richmond and with their combined forces launched an attack on June 26 that, in seven days of heavy fighting, drove the Union forces away from Richmond. The battle was a formidable success despite large Confederate casualties. Lee continued the offensive, shifting the campaign to northern Virginia, where he won another astonishing victory at Manassas on August 29-30, then crossed the Potomac for an invasion of Maryland. Meanwhile, Confederate armies in Tennessee also successfully invaded Kentucky in August.

This startling reversal of fortunes caused euphoria in the South and depression in the North. "The fatal blow has been dealt this 'grand army' of the North," wrote a Richmond diarist. "Lee has turned the tide, and I shall not be surprised if we have a long career of successes." In contrast, a New York diarist wrote: "The nation is rapidly sinking just now. Stonewall Jackson (our national bugaboo) about to invade Maryland, 40,000 strong. General advance of the rebel line threatening our hold on Missouri and Kentucky. Cincinnati in danger. Disgust with out present government certainly universal."

The governments of Britain and France, concluding that the

South had virtually established its independence with these military victories, were about to extend diplomatic recognition to the Confederacy—but held back pending the outcome of Lee's move into Maryland. Lee believed that even greater possibilities rode with his ragged legions as they began to ford the Potomac on September 4. On September 8, in a message that he sent to President Davis, Lee said, a "proposal of peace" backed by Southern armies on Union soil "would enable the people of the

ROBERT E. LEE STANDS BEFORE TWO FLAGS: THE SECOND NATIONAL CONFEDERATE FLAG (RIGHT) REPLACED THE ORIGINAL (LEFT), WHICH RESEMBLED THE U.S. FLAG AND CREATED CONFUSION IN BATTLE.

United States to determine at their coming [congressional] elections whether they will support those who favor a prolongation of the war, or those who wish to bring it to a termination [with] recognition of our independence."

These Confederate hopes were disappointed. Lee's Army of Northern Virginia was turned back in the bloody battle of Antietam on September 17. Three weeks later, Confederate General Braxton Bragg's Army of Tennessee suffered a similar fate at

the battle of Perryville in Kentucky. Both Confederate armies had to retreat with Union forces following closely behind as winter came on. Britain and France withheld diplomatic recognition, and Republicans retained their congressional majority in the Northern elections. During December, however, in three separate battles hundreds of miles apart, Union forces once again were roughly handled and had to suspend offensive operations: at Chickasaw Bluffs, near Vicksburg; at Murfreesboro, south of Nashville; and at Fredericksburg, halfway between Washington and Richmond.

Of these setbacks, the battle of Fredericksburg, on December 13, was the most dispiriting. Union troops made repeated assaults against entrenched Confederates only to be hurled back with 12,700 casualties (compared with 5,000 for the Confederates) to show for their efforts. Once again, Northern spirits plummeted. "The people have borne, silently and grimly, imbecility, treachery, failure, privation, loss of friends," declared the leading Northern magazine, *Harper's Weekly*, "but they cannot be expected to suffer that such massacres as this at Fredericksburg shall be repeated." When Lincoln heard the news of Fredericksburg, he said, "If there is a worse place than Hell, I am in it." One of the staunchest supporters of Lincoln's war policies, editor Joseph Medill of the *Chicago Tribune*, was profoundly depressed by the Union reverses in the winter of 1862-63. "An armistice is bound to come during this year," he wrote. "The rebs can't be conquered by the present machinery. We have to fight for a boundary. That is all now left to us."

Morale in Union armies, especially the Army of the Potomac, sank to its lowest point in the early months of 1863. Soldiers wrote home that "My loyalty is growing weak."—"I am sick and tired of disaster and the fools who bring disaster upon us." —"All think Virginia is not worth such a loss of life."—"Why not confess we are worsted, and come to an agreement?"

The Emancipation Proclamation had intensified

the sense of crisis. A Union sergeant wrote that the proclamation was "very, very unpopular in the army," for soldiers "think the cause of the Union has been dropped, and the cause of the Negro adopted . . . and all are anxious to return to their homes for it was to preserve the Union that they volunteered."

The future Supreme Court justice Oliver Wendell Holmes, Jr., a captain in a Massachusetts regiment who was recovering from the second of three war injuries, wrote dispiritedly that "the army is tired with its hard and terrible experience. . . . I've pretty much made up my mind that the South have achieved their independence."

The situation was to get worse before it got better. In his attempt to get at the Confederate bastion of Vicksburg, during the first four months of 1863, General Ulysses S. Grant seemed to be bogged down in the swamps and bayous of Mississippi and Louisiana. Thousands of his soldiers fell sick and many died. When criticism of the general mounted to a crescendo, Northern leaders put great pressure on Lincoln to get rid of Grant as a failure and a drunk. Lincoln stuck with him, even though, as he told a colleague, "I think Grant has hardly a friend left, except myself." But "what I want is generals who will fight and win battles and win victories. Grant has done this, and I propose to stand by him." It was at this time that Lincoln, in response to allegations about Grant's drinking, is reported to have said that he would like to know Grant's brand of whiskey so he could send some to his other generals.

Grant would soon justify Lincoln's confidence. Meanwhile, another Union general (with a more deserved reputation for drinking than Grant), Joseph Hooker, had taken command of the Army of the Potomac from Ambrose P. Burnside, who was discredited by the disaster at Fredericksburg. Hooker managed to revive morale. But his brash boasting got him into trouble. When Lincoln came down from Washington to visit the army on the Rappahannock in April 1863, Hooker told him that the question was not *whether* he would take Richmond, but *when*. "May God have mercy on General Lee," Hooker reportedly said, "for I will have none." Unhappy with this braggadocio, Lincoln was heard to remark that the hen was the wisest of all animal creation, for she never cackles until the egg is laid.

Hooker evidently missed the point. He launched

⭐ ⭐ ⭐ ⭐ ⭐

ROBERT E. LEE AFFECTIONATELY CALLED JAMES LONGSTREET "MY OLD WAR-HORSE," AN APT DESCRIPTION OF THIS CORPS COMMANDER WHO HELD AN UNBREAKABLE DEFENSIVE LINE AT ANTIETAM AND FREDERICKSBURG.

a well-conceived tactical movement, which got most of his army across the river in the rear of Lee's forces at Fredericksburg. On April 30, Hooker issued a congratulatory order to his men, "Our enemy must ingloriously fly, or come out from behind his defenses and give us battle on our own ground, where certain destruction awaits him." But when Lee decided to give battle rather than fly ingloriously, Hooker lost his nerve, lost the initiative, and lost the ensuing battle of Chancellorsville.

This battle marked Lee's most brilliant achievement. Facing odds of almost two to one (General James Longstreet was with two divisions in a minor campaign south of Norfolk), Lee divided his army three times in a series of flanking maneuvers and tactical assaults that bewildered Hooker. The key to Jackson's victory was a long flank march to attack and rout the Union right. The initiative was a smashing success, but it cost Jackson an arm when he was shot by a detachment of Confederate troops that mistook him and his staff for Union cavalry in the moonlit woods. When Lee heard the news, he said that Jackson "has lost his left arm; but I have lost my right arm." Eight days later Jackson died of pneumonia, which set in after he was wounded.

This setback only briefly tempered the joy and confidence in the Confederacy produced by the victory at Chancellorsville. Southerners believed that independence was all but achieved. The mood in the North seemed to confirm this conviction. When Lincoln learned of the outcome of Chancellorsville his face turned "ashen," according to a newspaper reporter who was present at the War Department telegraph office. "My God, my God," Lincoln exclaimed. "What will the country say?" It said plenty, and nearly all of it bad. Copperheads turned up the volume of their talk about the failure of the war and the need for an armistice. Republicans were stunned. When the influential Senator Charles Sumner of Massachusetts heard the news of Chancellorsville, he cried out, "Lost, lost, all is lost."

But despite their great victory in Virginia, Confederates faced peril on other fronts. In Mississippi, Grant had begun the drive that would pen Vicksburg's defenders into their works for a siege. The Union army in middle Tennessee stood poised for a possible advance. A combined task force of Union troops and ships had launched a series of attacks on Charleston. And in Virginia, Hooker's army of ninety thousand men still occupied the north bank of the Rappahannock despite its defeat at Chancellorsville. All around its perimeter, the Confederacy was menaced by larger forces that spelled danger.

These forces also spelled opportunity if the South could convert the momentum of Chancellorsville into an offensive that would relieve the pressure and perhaps win another battle that would knock the North out of the war. Southern leaders knew that their friends in Britain and France had revived the movement for diplomatic recognition. They were also aware of the growing

power of the antiwar Copperheads in the North. Another big victory might win the dual prizes of European and Northern recognition of the Confederacy's independence.

A flurry of telegrams and conferences in Richmond among the Confederacy's top generals, the Cabinet, and President Davis canvassed various strategic plans. Returning from southside Virginia with his two detached divisions (commanded by John Bell Hood and George Pickett), Longstreet proposed a plan to take these divisions to middle Tennessee to reinforce General Braxton Bragg. They would launch an offensive to recapture Nashville, clear the Yankees out of Tennessee, and drive northward to the Ohio River. The attack might force Grant to loosen his grip on Vicksburg if he attempted to aid the retreating Yankees. Davis and Secretary of War James Seddon liked the idea but suggested a modification: Longstreet's two divisions would reinforce Vicksburg directly, drive Grant away, and then push into Tennessee to help Bragg.

Lee did not like either plan. The Southern railroad system was too rickety to transport fifteen thousand troops that far west in time for them to do any good, he said. The heat and diseases of a deep-South summer would force unacclimated Northern troops in Mississippi to retreat anyway. Without Longstreet's divisions, Lee warned, he might have to pull back into the Richmond defenses. Perhaps, he hinted darkly, it would "become a question between [losing] Virginia and Mississippi."

At a crucial strategy conference in Richmond on May 15, Lee dazzled Davis and the Cabinet with a bold vision. He would invade Pennsylvania with a reinforced Army of Northern Virginia and inflict a demoralizing defeat on the Yankees in their own backyard. This would remove the enemy threat on the Rappahannock, take the armies out of war-ravaged Virginia, enable Confederates to supply themselves from the rich Pennsylvania countryside, and relieve the pressure on Confederate armies in the west

LONGSTREET AND HIS STAFF WERE NON-VIRGINIANS IN THE ARMY OF NORTHERN VIRGINIA. AT TIMES THIS CAUSED TENSE RELATIONS WITH THE OTHER COMMAND STAFFS, MOST OF WHOM WERE VIRGINIANS, BECAUSE LONSTREET HAD A STRATEGIC VISION THAT ENCOMPASSED THE WHOLE CONFEDERACY, WHILE MANY OF THE VIRGINIANS FOCUSED MAINLY ON THEIR NATIVE STATE.

by compelling Union forces there to send reinforcements to the east. Lee's plan would also strengthen the Northern Copperheads' arguments for peace, discredit Lincoln and his war policies, encourage European diplomatic recognition of the Confederacy—perhaps even capture Baltimore or Harrisburg and hold them hostage for a cease-fire and peace negotiations.

The Cabinet was awed by these prospects. In the post-Chancellorsville aura of invincibility, anything seemed possible for the Army of Northern Virginia. "There never were such men in an army before," Lee said of his soldiers. "They will go anywhere and do anything if properly led." So great was the prestige of Lee, "whose fame," said a Cabinet member, "now filled the world," that he carried the day. Even Longstreet came around. "When I agreed with [Secretary of War] Seddon and yourself about sending troops west," he wrote to Senator Louis Wigfall of Texas, "it was under the impression that we would be obliged to remain on the defensive here. But the prospect of an advance changes the aspect of affairs."

In later years Longstreet claimed that his original idea of reinforcing the western armies would have been better. Several historians have also criticized Lee for his narrow preoccupation with Virginia. As a Virginian who had opposed secession until his own state left the Union, Lee had gone to war with the motive of defending his state. He is said to have lacked a large strategic vision encompassing the Confederacy as a whole. The same might be said of his principal subordinates. Longstreet was the only corps commander in Lee's army who was not a Virginian. After the death of Jackson (a Virginian), Lee had reorganized the army by dividing Jackson's old corps in two and assigning the commands to Richard Ewell and A. P. Hill (both Virginians). Stuart (a Virginian) commanded the cavalry corps. An extraordinary five of the nine commanders of infantry divisions were also

Virginians. The charge of narrow and excessive concern with Virginia while the Yankees overran the western Confederate states therefore had some basis in fact. Yet, had it not been for Lee's remarkable tactical victories in Virginia during the previous year, the South might already have lost the war. And had the Confederates won the ensuing battle of Gettysburg, nothing would ever have been heard of the defects in Lee's strategic vision.

Having reorganized and rested his army during the month after Chancellorsville, Lee headed toward the Shenandoah Valley during the first week of June. He intended to use the Blue Ridge and South Mountain ranges to protect his right flank as he penetrated into Maryland and Pennsylvania. Only one event marred the early days of the campaign. On June 9 a large Union cavalry force crossed the Rappahannock to attack Stuart's cavalry at Brandy Station. With the advantage of surprise, the blue troopers achieved initial success, dealing out more punishment to the gray horsemen than they had experienced in the war thus far. Some of the best fighting was done by a Union division under Brigadier General John Buford. A native of Kentucky, Buford remained loyal to the flag he had served for nearly twenty years while a brother and a cousin became generals in the Confederate army.

Stuart's troopers eventually blunted the Union assault and, reinforced by infantry, finally forced the Yankees back across the Rappahannock. But in subsequent days the Richmond press criticized Stuart and his "puffed-up cavalry" for having been surprised and roughly handled at Brandy Station. Stuart's ego was bruised. He had won deserved fame for his daring exploits and accurate scouting reports during the previous year. Many people quoted his *bon mot* about his father-in-law, Philip St. George Cooke, a Virginian who stayed with the Union and commanded a Northern cavalry brigade. "He will

★ ★ ★ ★ ★ ★

MOST CIVIL WAR FIELD GUNS HAD AN EFFECTIVE RANGE OF A MILE OR LESS AND WERE OF DUBIOUS ACCURACY AT ANY DISTANCE GREATER THAN HALF A MILE. THEY WERE THEREFORE MOST DEVASTATING AT CLOSE RANGE, FIRING GRAPE OR CANISTER (LIKE A GIANT SHOTGUN) AGAINST CHARGING INFANTRY. UNION ARTILLERY HELPED BREAK UP PICKETT'S CHARGE AT GETTYSBURG IN THIS MANNER.

regret it but once," Stuart had said of this decision, "and that will be continuously."

Stuart dressed the part of a dashing cavalier: knee-high boots, elbow-length gauntlets, a red-lined cape with a yellow sash, and a felt hat with pinned-up brim and ostrich-feather plume. After Brandy Station, he was determined to dispel criticism and live up to his reputation with some new bold and dramatic deed. Two weeks later an opportunity arose. After screening the Confederate infantry's advance northward by defending the Blue Ridge passes from Union cavalry probes, Stuart got permission from Lee to move into Pennsylvania, provided he always remain in contact with the main body of infantry. This Stuart failed to do. When he took his three best cavalry brigades on another raid around the rear of the northward-slogging Union army, he became separated from the Army of Northern Virginia for a full week, depriving Lee of his cavalry "eyes" at a crucial time.

Nevertheless, these hot June days seemed to signify the pinnacle of Confederate success. On June 14-15, Ewell's corps achieved a spectacular victory by capturing thirty-five hundred Union troops defending Winchester. This seemed to mark Ewell as a worthy successor to Jackson. He rivaled Jackson in eccentricity, with his ulcer-induced diet of hulled wheat in milk with raisins and an egg yolk, his beaked nose, and his habit of cocking his head to one side, which reminded observers of a bird. Ewell had recently married a widow, whom he referred to absent-mindedly as "Mrs. Brown." He had lost a leg at Second Manassas the previous August and had returned to duty with a wooden leg—which may have diluted the aggressiveness he showed as Jackson's subordinate. Ewell's planning of the attack at Winchester had been careful and its execution methodical. This had led to success, but the same cautious approach would reap different results at Gettysburg.

As the Confederates marched north, Lee wrote a letter to Davis outlining the political results that he

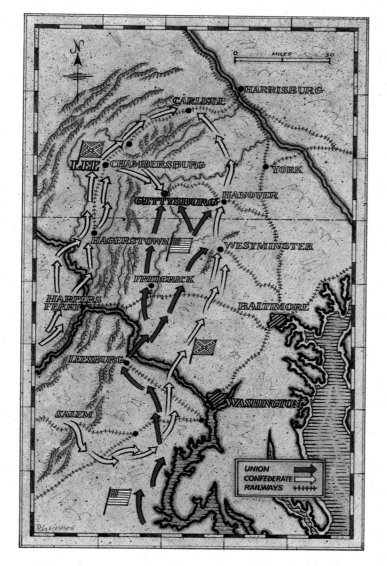

★ ★ ★ ★ ★ ★ ★ ★ ★ ★ ★ ★ ★ ★

hoped military success in Pennsylvania would bring. Lee placed great faith in what he described as "the rising peace party of the North" as a "means of weakening and dividing our enemies." It was true, Lee acknowledged, that the Copperheads professed to regard reunion as the object of peace negotiations while the Confederates regarded independence as the goal. But it might be desirable, Lee advised Davis, to play along with the idea of negotiations in order to help the Peace Democrats undermine the Northern will to continue fighting, which "after all is what we are interested in bringing about. When peace is proposed to us it will be time enough to discuss its terms, and it is not the part of prudence to spurn the proposition in advance, merely because those who made it believe, or affect to believe, that it will result in bringing us back to the Union." Confident that Davis agreed with these views, Lee wrote that "you will best know how to give effect to them."

Davis did indeed think he saw a chance to carry peace proposals on the point of Lee's sword. In mid-June, Confederate Vice-President Alexander Stephens suggested to Davis that in light of the "failure of Hooker and Grant," this was the time to make peace overtures. Stephens offered to approach Lincoln (with whom he had served in Congress as a fellow Whig in the 1840s) under flag of truce to discuss prisoner-of-war exchanges, which had broken down because of Confederate refusal to exchange captured black soldiers. Davis was intrigued by the idea. He gave Stephens formal instructions authorizing him to negotiate the exchanges—and perhaps informal authority to negotiate peace when news of Lee's victory on Northern soil reached Washington. On July 3 Stephens boarded a flag-of-truce boat for a voyage down the James River on the first leg of his trip to Washington.

By that time, reports of Lee's initial success in Pennsylvania elated people in the South (accurate news took several days to reach Richmond). This proved "the easy susceptibility of the North to invasion," gloated the *Richmond Examiner*. "We can carry our armies far into the enemy's country, exacting peace by blows leveled at his vitals."

Lee exuded similar confidence. On June 28 most of his army was at Chambersburg while elements of Ewell's corps were at York and Carlisle and near the south bank of the Susquehanna River threatening Harrisburg. Although Lee was troubled by Stuart's absence, leaving him without accurate intelligence about the enemy's whereabouts, he nevertheless told one of his subordinates that when the Army of the Potomac came up into Pennsylvania

seeking him, "I shall throw an overwhelming force on their advance, crush it, follow up the success, drive one corps back on another, and by successive repulses and surprises create a panic and virtually destroy the army. [Then] the war will be over and we shall achieve the recognition of our independence."

This was the pride that goeth before a fall. The Army of the Potomac was coming, with more speed and élan than Lee realized. The army also had a new commander. When the Confederates moved north, Lincoln saw opportunity in this apparent threat, opportunity to cut off and cripple the enemy far from his home base. Lincoln told Secretary of the Navy Gideon Welles that "we cannot help beating them, if we have the man." But Lincoln became convinced that Hooker was not the man. The general had begun to fret that Lee outnumbered him, that he needed more troops, and that the government was not supporting him. To Lincoln this sounded like Hooker was afraid to fight Lee again. When the general submitted his resignation over a quarrel about the Union garrison at Harpers Ferry, Lincoln accepted it and appointed a surprised George Gordon Meade to command on June 28.

Meade was the fifth commander of the Army of the Potomac. He had compiled a solid if not brilliant record as a division and corps commander; his division was the only one to achieve a temporary breakthrough at Fredericksburg. Meade's testy temper and piercing eyes, crowned by a high forehead, caused one soldier to describe him as "a God-damned old goggle-eyed snapping turtle." But Meade's tactical skill, including the effective use of terrain and

reserves, would play a large part in the coming battle.

As the Army of the Potomac headed north into Pennsylvania, civilians along the way cheered the men as friends instead of reviling them as foes. The soldiers' morale rose with the latitude. "Our men are three times as enthusiastic as they have been in Virginia," wrote a Union surgeon. "The idea that Pennsylvania is invaded and that we are fighting on our own soil proper, influences them strongly. They are more determined than I have ever before seen them."

These soldiers had been toughened in earlier campaigns under fumbling leaders to a flinty self-reliance. They "have something of the English bull-dog in them," wrote one officer. "You can whip them time and again, but the next fight they go into, they are as full of pluck as ever . . . Some day or other we shall have our turn." That day was coming soon.

On the night of June 28, one of Longstreet's scouts brought word that the Army of the Potomac was concentrated just south of the Maryland line and moving north. With no word from Stuart, Lee was forced to act quickly on this information lest he be caught with his forces divided. He sent couriers to recall Ewell's divisions from York and Carlisle. Meanwhile, one of A. P. Hill's divisions learned of a reported supply of shoes at Gettysburg, a prosperous market town of twenty-five hundred people served by a dozen roads that converged from every point of the compass. Since Lee intended to unite his army near Gettysburg, which was reported to be defended by nothing but local militia, on July 1 Hill authorized his division to go there and "get those shoes."

THE WORLD CAN NEVER FORGET WHAT THEY DID HERE

PART · TWO

THE ADVANCE UNITS OF A. P. HILL'S CORPS WERE IN FOR A SURPRISE ON THAT FATEFUL JULY 1. THE TROOPS ON A RIDGE TWO MILES NORTHWEST OF GETTYSBURG WERE NOT MILITIA. THEY WERE TWO BRIGADES OF JOHN BUFORD'S CAVALRY, WHICH HAD FOUGHT SO WELL AT BRANDY STATION THREE WEEKS EARLIER.

AT GETTYSBURG THEY FOUGHT DISMOUNTED—A TACTIC INCREASINGLY PREVALENT DURING THE CIVIL WAR, WHEN RIFLED, INSTEAD OF SMOOTHBORE, MUSKETS MADE CAVALRY CHARGES AGAINST INFANTRY SUICIDALLY OBSOLETE. ONE OF EVERY FOUR TROOPERS HELD

★ ★

"WITHOUT MUSIC WE COULDN'T HAVE AN ARMY," SAID ROBERT E. LEE. IN THE FIRST YEAR OF THE WAR, MANY REGIMENTS HAD BANDS AND MUSICIANS WHO ALSO SERVED AS STRETCHER BEARERS IN BATTLE. BY 1863, MEN WERE NEEDED TO CARRY GUNS RATHER THAN TO PLAY HORNS AND, ESPECIALLY IN THE CONFEDERATE ARMY, MOST REGIMENTAL BANDS DISAPPEARED OR WERE CONSOLIDATED INTO BRIGADE BANDS.

> *"They will attack in the morning and they will come booming—skirmishers three-deep. We will have to fight like the devil until supports arrive."*
>
> *—Buford on June 30, 1863*

A NATIVE OF KEN-
TUCKY, JOHN BUFORD
MOVED TO ILLINOIS
AS A TEEN-AGER
AND SPENT THIR-
TEEN YEARS AS A
CAVALRYMAN ON
THE WESTERN
PLAINS BEFORE
JOINING THE UNION
ARMY IN 1861. A
BROTHER AND A
COUSIN FOUGHT
FOR THE OPPOSING
SIDE AND BECAME
CONFEDERATE
GENERALS.

four horses while his three comrades fought. Though they numbered only twenty-five hundred men against seven thousand in the division commanded by Henry Heth, Hill's senior brigadier, the Yankees had one advantage. Like most Union horse soldiers, they were armed by this stage of the war with Sharps single-shot breech-loading carbines or seven-shot Spencer repeating carbines. Infantrymen carried single-shot Springfield or Enfield muzzle-loading rifles. These weapons had a longer range than cavalry carbines, but even a good infantryman could get off only two or three shots a minute, while a trooper armed with a Sharps carbine could fire almost twice as fast and one armed with a Spencer repeater faster yet. Union cavalry had this technological and indus-

★ ★ ★ ★ ★ ★ ★ ★ ★ ★ ★ ★ ★ ★ ★ ★ ★ ★ ★ ★

ON JUNE 30, THE EVE OF THE BATTLE OF GETTYSBURG, GENERAL
JOHN BUFORD (WALKING IN FRONT OF THE GETTYSBURG SEMINARY)
CONTEMPLATES THE ENEMY POSITION AND PREPARES FOR THE NEXT
DAY'S BATTLE. LATER THE SEMINARY WAS TURNED INTO A MAKESHIFT
HOSPITAL FOR THE WOUNDED. (PAGES 30–31) BUFORD LEADS HIS STAFF
INTO POSITION NEAR THE SEMINARY AT DAWN ON JULY 1.

trial advantage by the third year of the war (Union infantry, however, remained equipped with muzzle-loaders), especially in the dismounted skirmishing tactics used by Buford's troopers that morning.

Buford directed the action from the cupola of a building at the Lutheran seminary, which gave its name to another ridge a mile closer to town. For two hours, from 8:00 to 10:00 A.M., these Yankee cavalrymen and one artillery battery held back probing attacks by Heth's division. Using fence rails, trees, and the contours of the ground for cover, the troopers fell back from one ridge to the next, forcing Heth to deploy repeatedly. Meanwhile, Buford sent couriers pounding down the road to summon General John Reynolds, commander of the Union 1st Corps. Buford recognized the ridges and rocky hills around Gettysburg as ideal defensive terrain for a battle. When Reynolds arrived at about 10:00 A.M. at the head of his corps, followed closely by the 11th Corps, he agreed with Buford. Reynolds deployed his troops along a ridge west of town and sent Major General Oliver O. Howard out to the more level terrain north of town to meet Ewell's corps, reported to be approaching from the north.

When General Heth mounted an all-out attack in late morning, he expected to run over Buford's outnumbered and tired cavalry. Instead, he got another unpleasant surprise. He ran into Union infantry, including the famous Iron Brigade, the only all-western brigade in the Army of the Potomac (three regiments from Wisconsin and one each from Indiana and Michigan). Although the Iron Brigade suffered heavy casualties, these veterans upheld their reputation as the toughest unit in the army. One of the casualties, however, was Reynolds himself, killed instantly with a shot through the head as he was deploying the Iron Brigade.

A few minutes after Reynolds's death, two Iron Brigade regiments swept into the right flank of Brigadier General James J. Archer's brigade of Tennesseeans and Alabamians, capturing many of the men plus Archer himself. Archer thus became the first of

★ ★

RIFLED MUSKETS HAD GREATER RANGE AND ACCURACY THAN THE
SMOOTHBORE MUSKETS USED IN PREVIOUS WARS, MAKING CAVALRY
CHARGES AGAINST INFANTRY SUICIDAL. SMART CAVALRY COMMANDERS
LIKE BUFORD TRAINED THEIR MEN TO FIGHT DISMOUNTED, USING THE
COVER OF WOODS, CONTOURS IN THE GROUND, OR THE BARRICADES OF
FENCE RAILS. ON THE MORNING OF JULY 1, ONE OF EVERY FOUR MEN
HELD THE HORSES IN THE REAR WHILE THEIR COMRADES, ARMED WITH
BREECH-LOADING CARBINES, FOUGHT OFF PROBING CONFEDERATE
INFANTRY ATTACKS AS BUFORD AND HIS STAFF WATCHED THE ACTION.

Lee's generals to suffer the ignominy of capture during the war. Grinning, a big Union private named Patrick Maloney escorted a scowling Archer roughly to the rear. Behind the lines, Archer and Maloney ran into Brigadier General Abner Doubleday, who had succeeded Reynolds as commander of the corps. Archer and Doubleday had been friends in the old army. "Archer! I'm glad to see you," said Doubleday as he strode forward to shake hands. "Well, I'm not glad to see you by a damn sight," growled Archer as he turned away.

By early afternoon the Union forces had repulsed Heth's attacks. As Lee had ridden toward Gettysburg with Longstreet that morning, they had heard the rumbling of artillery from ten or twelve miles away. Lee was puzzled and disturbed. He had ordered Hill not to bring on a battle until the whole army was concentrated. Lee had no cavalry to keep him informed of what was happening up ahead. "I cannot think what has become of Stuart," he said in irritation. "I ought to have heard from him before now. . . . I am in ignorance of what we have in front of us here. It may be the whole Federal army, it may be only a detachment. If it is the whole Federal force, we must fight a battle here." Lee bid farewell to Longstreet, whose corps brought up the rear, and rode ahead toward the guns of Gettysburg to find out what was going on.

Lee arrived a little after 2:00 P.M. to discover Hill preparing for a new attack. From north of town came the sounds of fighting.

Two of Ewell's divisions had arrived and had immediately gone into action against the right flank of the Union 1st Corps and two divisions of the IIth. Lee was still reluctant to unleash Hill until Longstreet, several miles away, could come up. But the battle was out of Lee's hands. The Confederates outnumbered the two Union corps that were in the vicinity (Confederate divisions were larger than Union divisions). As Ewell's attack went forward, Lee finally told Hill to go in.

An hour's concentrated fighting finally broke the Union lines, starting on the right with the ill-fated IIth Corps (nicknamed the "Dutch Corps" because many of its regiments were composed of German-Americans), which had buckled under Jackson's onslaught at Chancellorsville. It buckled again here,

★ ★ ★ ★ ★ ★

WHEN JOHN REY-
NOLDS ARRIVED AT
GETTYSBURG ON THE
MORNING OF JULY 1,
HE FOUND GENERAL
BUFORD IN THE
SEMINARY CUPOLA.

mainly because Jubal Early's division of Ewell's corps had arrived on a road that brought them in on the right flank of the IIth Corps, causing it to cave in from right to left, despite the heroics of Captain Hubert Dilger, commander of a six-gun artillery battery in the corps. A native of Germany, known as "Leatherbreeches" because of the doeskin trousers he liked to wear, Dilger was one of the best artillerists in the Union army, bold and fearless in getting his guns close to the enemy. But even Dilger's rapid-firing cannons could do little to stem the rout as thousands of bluecoats surrendered and the rest swarmed through Gettysburg toward a hill south of town. One IIth Corps brigade commander, with the mellifluous name of Alexander Schimmelfennig, saved himself from capture by hiding for three days in a pigsty—an experience from which his reputation never recovered.

The commander of the IIth Corps was Major General Oliver O. Howard, a pious Congregationalist from Maine who, like his adversary Richard Ewell, had lost a limb earlier in the war—in Howard's case an arm. Howard had kept one division in reserve on the high ground a half mile south of town known as Cemetery Hill, because the town burial ground was located there. Howard fortified the hill with artillery and rifle pits, occupied by his reserve division, as a rallying point for Union troops if they were driven back—a foresighted action for which Howard later received the official Thanks of Congress. It remains unrecorded whether Howard or anyone else appreciated the irony of a sign on the cemetery gate: "All persons found using firearms in these grounds will be prosecuted with the utmost rigor of the law." The survivors of the 1st Corps and IIth Corps did rally on Cemetery Hill and on another rise, Culp's Hill, a half mile to the east.

This stopped the retreat. Nevertheless, it appeared that the Confederates had won another victory. Lee knew, however, that the victory was incomplete so long as Union forces held those hills. He also knew

THE CUPOLA ATOP THIS LUTHERAN SEMINARY BUILDING, WHICH STILL STANDS TODAY, WAS BUFORD'S OBSERVATION POST ON THE MORNING OF JULY 1. CONFEDERATE OFFICERS USED IT FOR THE SAME PURPOSE ON JULY 2 AND 3.

that the rest of the Army of the Potomac must be hurrying toward Gettysburg; his best chance was to drive the remnants of the 1st Corps and 11th Corps off the high ground before they got there. For this he turned to Ewell, whose corps had suffered less damage than Hill's during the day's fighting. Three hours of daylight remained. Lee gave verbal orders to Ewell to attack Cemetery Hill "if practicable."

Ewell reconnoitered the position, consulted subordinates, and then hesitated. His troops were tired and disorganized from chasing Yankees through town and rounding up prisoners. They were suffering from lack of water on a hot day after a long march and intense fighting. Ewell could see in the fading light that the Union position on Cemetery Hill was formidable; he suspected correctly that it was being reinforced by newly arriving troops. So he decided that it was not practicable to attack.

Because the Confederates failed to take Cemetery Hill on July 1, Union troops were able to consolidate their position on the hill and on the ridge running south of it during the night. Ewell's failure to attack has thus been the subject of much criticism. It has been one of the biggest of many "ifs" concerning the battle of Gettysburg through the years. *If* Jackson had still been alive, would he have attacked? And *if* he—or Ewell—had done so, would the Confederates have carried the position? The answer to the first question is probably yes; the answer to the second is far less certain. Ewell could have sent no more than seven or eight thousand men of his own corps into such an attack, and Lee had told him he could expect no support from any other part of the army. Union forces had considerably more than eight thousand troops to defend the hill, dug in and less disorganized than critics of Ewell assume them to have been. It may well be that Ewell made the right decision. In any case, as the leading historian of the

AS REYNOLDS GALLOPED UP TO SEMINARY RIDGE AT 10:00 A.M. ON JULY 1, BUFORD POINTED TO THE CONFEDERATE INFANTRY FORMING FOR AN ALL-OUT ATTACK ON HIS CAVALRY. "THERE'S THE DEVIL TO PAY!" SAID BUFORD. REYNOLDS SENT IN HIS BEST UNIT, THE IRON BRIGADE, TO STOP THE ATTACK BUT WAS KILLED AS HE DIRECTED ITS DEPLOYMENT.

battle (Edward Coddington, *The Gettysburg Campaign*) notes, "Responsibility for the failure of the Confederates to make an all-out assault on Cemetery Hill on July 1 must rest with Lee." He was the commanding general. He was present on the ground. If he wanted an attack, he should have ordered and organized it.

Perhaps Lee recognized this, for the next morning he was eager to attack. The whole army was united, except for Pickett's division, still back at Chambersburg, and Stuart's cavalry, which had finally turned up at Carlisle, a day's ride to the north. Longstreet joined Lee on the morning of July 2 as they gazed at the Union lines through binoculars.

All but one corps of the Army of the Potomac had arrived during the night, and that one was on its way by forced marches. The Union defensive position occupied high ground south of Gettysburg in a

⋆ ⋆ ⋆ ⋆ ⋆ ⋆ ⋆ ⋆ ⋆ ⋆ ⋆ ⋆ ⋆ ⋆ ⋆

THE DARING TACTICS OF GERMAN-BORN HUBERT DILGER, COMMANDER OF A BATTERY OF OHIO ARTILLERY, SLOWED BUT COULD NOT STOP THE CONFEDERATE BREAKTHROUGH ON THE UNION RIGHT. A YEAR LATER, AFTER THE 11TH CORPS HAD BEEN TRANSFERRED TO THE GEORGIA THEATER, A SHOT FROM ONE OF DILGER'S GUNS KILLED LIEUTENANT GENERAL LEONIDAS POLK, THE SECOND HIGHEST-RANKING CONFEDERATE KILLED IN THE WAR.

line whose shape resembled an upside-down fish-hook with the curved end of the hook on Culp's and Cemetery hills and the shank running two miles south along Cemetery Ridge to the eye of the hook on the rocky prominence of Little Round Top. This was a strong position. Not only did it command high ground, but its convex shape, with the flanks only two miles apart, enabled troops to be shifted quickly from one place to another to reinforce weak spots. By contrast, the Confederate concave exterior lines made communication between the widely separated flanks slow and difficult.

A master of defensive tactics, Longstreet recognized the strength of the Union position. At Second Manassas the previous August, he had commanded the right half of the Army of Northern Virginia and had stood on the defensive until Union forces had exhausted themselves attacking Jackson's corps on his left. Longstreet then unleashed a devastating counterattack that won the battle. At Antietam he had commanded the Confederate center and right, holding firm on the defensive to prevent any breakthrough by superior enemy numbers and helping to save the army from serious peril. At Fredericksburg, Longstreet's superb defense of Marye's Heights had decimated Union assaults. In fact, all of Longstreet's successes had come in defensive fighting—followed, in the case of Second Manassas, by a counterattack.

Defensive fighting also seemed to fit Longstreet's personality. Regarded by some as ponderous and phlegmatic, he was in reality reflective and sagacious. He was more aware than many of his contemporaries that courage and dash could not overcome the strength of entrenched defenders possessing rifles with an accurate range four times greater than

ON THE EVENING OF JULY 1, BEGINNING AN ALL-NIGHT FORCED MARCH, JOSHUA LAWRENCE CHAMBERLAIN, A COLONEL OF INFANTRY, LED HIS REGIMENT, THE 20TH MAINE, TO GETTYSBURG, WHERE HE WOULD WIN THE CONGRESSIONAL MEDAL OF HONOR.

(PAGES 44–45) AS LEE RODE INTO GETTYSBURG ON THE EVENING OF JULY 1, HIS TROOPS CHEERED IN CELEBRATION OF THE BATTLE THEY ASSUMED THEY HAD WON. BUT LEE KNEW THE VICTORY WAS NOT COMPLETE SO LONG AS UNION FORCES HELD THE HILLS AND RIDGES SOUTH OF TOWN. AS HE WAITED FOR LONGSTREET'S CORPS TO ARRIVE, LEE PLANNED HOW HE MIGHT ATTACK THOSE HEIGHTS ON THE MORROW.

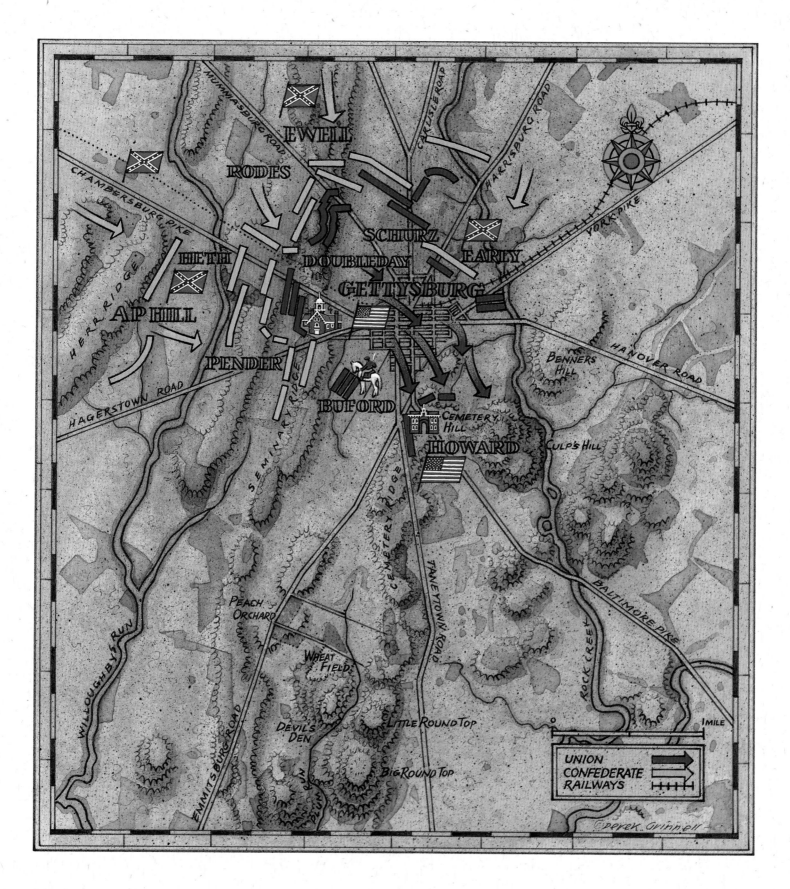

EWELL

RODES

CHAMBERSBURG PIKE

MUMMASBURG ROAD

CARLISLE ROAD

HARRISBURG ROAD

YORK PIKE

HETH

SCHURZ

DOUBLEDAY

EARLY

AP HILL

GETTYSBURG

HERR RIDGE

PENDER

HAGERSTOWN ROAD

SEMINARY RIDGE

BUFORD

HOWARD

BENNERS HILL

HANOVER ROAD

CEMETERY HILL

CULP'S HILL

CEMETERY RIDGE

TANEYTOWN ROAD

ROCK CREEK

BALTIMORE PIKE

WILLOUGHBY RUN

EMMITSBURG ROAD

PEACH ORCHARD

WHEAT FIELD

DEVIL'S DEN

PLUM RUN

Little Round Top

Big Round Top

0   1 mile

UNION
CONFEDERATE
RAILWAYS

©Derek Grinnell

the smoothbore muskets of the Napoleonic Wars or the Mexican War, in which many senior Civil War officers had fought.

As Longstreet studied the Union position on the morning of July 2, he therefore concluded that it was too strong for an attack to prevail. He urged Lee to make a flanking move several miles to the south and find some good defensive terrain between Gettysburg and Washington. This maneuver would compel Meade (who had arrived at Gettysburg the preceding night) to attack the Confederates, who could then stand on the defensive and repeat the triumph of Fredericksburg or Second Manassas. But Lee rejected this advice. The model of a successful battle he had most vividly in mind was Chancellorsville, where just two months before courage and dash—plus some dazzling tactical maneuvers by Lee and Jackson—had enabled them to overcome superior numbers by *attacking*, not by fighting defensively. Longstreet, of course, had not been at Chancellorsville. Nor had he arrived at Gettysburg on July I in time to see Hill's and Ewell's divisions drive the Yankees pell-mell through the town.

Lee wanted to continue the momentum. He was ready for a fight. The morale of his troops had never been higher. According to Colonel Arthur Fremantle, a British observer accompanying the Army of Northern Virginia, the men were eager to attack an enemy "they had beaten so constantly" and for whose fighting capacity they felt "profound contempt." They might regard the move that Longstreet suggested as a retreat and lose their edge. With limited supplies and a vulnerable line of communications to the South, Lee could not stay in Pennsylvania indefinitely. He had come there to win a battle; he intended to do so that day. Pointing to Cemetery Hill, he told Longstreet, "The enemy is there, and I am going to attack him there."

Longstreet replied, "If he is there, it will be because he is anxious that we should attack him; a good reason, in my judgment, for not doing so."

⭐ ⭐ ⭐ ⭐ ⭐ ⭐

THE ACTION ON JULY 1 WAS CONCENTRATED IN THE AREA HIGHLIGHTED IN THE MAP (LEFT). THE GRAY ARROWS WEST AND NORTH OF TOWN INDICATE LINES OF CONFEDERATE ATTACK, WHICH IN THE LATE AFTERNOON DROVE UNION TROOPS (BLUE ARROWS) THROUGH THE TOWN OF GETTYSBURG AND BACK TO A NEW POSITION ON CEMETERY HILL. (RIGHT) DRUMMERS IN THE CIVIL WAR ARMIES WERE MOSTLY BOYS, SOME AS YOUNG AS TWELVE. ONE OF THE FUNCTIONS OF THE DRUMMERS AND BUGLERS WAS TO SOUND THE SIGNALS THAT INSTRUCTED TROOPS TO CHANGE FORMATIONS DURING BATTLE. THE DEAFENING NOISE OF DOZENS OF CANNONS AND THOUSANDS OF RIFLES OFTEN MADE EVEN THE PIERCING NOTES OF BUGLES AND THE LOUD RATTLE OF DRUMS ALMOST INAUDIBLE, SO THAT ORDERS HAD TO BE CARRIED BY COURIER AND SHOUTED TO UNITS AT CLOSE RANGE.

But Lee had made up his mind. Longstreet turned away sadly, he wrote in an account of the battle years later, with a conviction of impending disaster.

Lee's strategy was to attack both flanks. Ewell still thought that the Union right on Cemetery and Culp's hills was too strong, so Lee ordered Longstreet to take his two divisions (the third, Pickett's, was still on the way) plus Hill's one division that had not fought the previous day and attack the Union left. Ewell would demonstrate against the enemy in his front and convert the demonstration into a real attack if Meade weakened that flank to reinforce his left against Longstreet's assault.

Longstreet took a long time to get his troops into position for the attack. A large part of the delay was not his fault. The absence of cavalry had made scouting a route to the jump-off point difficult. Because the Confederates wanted the attack to be a surprise, Longstreet had been forced to countermarch for several miles, after discovering that the original road to the attack point was in view of a Union signal station on Little Round Top.

Part of Longstreet's slowness on July 2 may have resulted from a lack of enthusiasm for the attack he had been ordered to make. After the war, Longstreet

ON THE AFTERNOON OF JULY 2, WILLIAM BARKSDALE, AN ANTEBELLUM CONGRESSMAN FROM MISSISSIPPI AND A FIERY SECESSIONIST, LED HIS BRIGADE IN A VICTORIOUS CHARGE AT GETTYSBURG. IN THE BATTLE, 50 PERCENT OF THE MEN LOST THEIR LIVES, INCLUDING BARKSDALE.

became a target of withering criticism by the Virginians who gained control of Confederate historiography. They accused him of insubordination and tardiness at Gettysburg. They held him responsible for losing the battle—and, by implication, the war. But some of this criticism was self-serving, intended to shield Lee and other Virginians (chiefly Ewell and Stuart) from blame.

In any event, Longstreet finally got into position by midafternoon. But he did not find the Yankee left on Cemetery Ridge, where it had been earlier in the day. It was not there because of an unauthorized move by Major General Daniel E. Sickles, commander of the 3rd Corps, holding the Union left. Dan Sickles was one of the more colorful characters in a war that abounded with flamboyant types. Sickles was a "political general"—a category more prevalent in both armies than the professionals desired—someone who was commissioned because of his political influence rather than for his military qualifications. At Gettysburg, however, Sickles was the only nonprofessional (that is, not a West Point graduate)

★ ★ ★ ★ ★ ★ ★ ★ ★ ★ ★ ★ ★ ★ ★

IN THE LATE AFTERNOON OF JULY 2, A CONFEDERATE BRIGADE WAS POISED TO CAPTURE THE UNDEFENDED LITTLE ROUND TOP, THE KEY TO THE UNION LEFT ON CEMETERY RIDGE. A UNION BRIGADE HEADED BY THE 20TH MAINE RACED TO THE CREST JUST IN TIME TO STOP THE CONFEDERATES.

commanding a corps on either side. Sickles was a stalwart of the Tammany Hall machine in New York City. While a congressman in 1859, he shot and killed his wife's lover, who happened to be the son of Francis Scott Key, author of "The Star Spangled Banner." Sickles's trial ended in acquittal on the grounds of temporary insanity—the first use of that defense in the history of American jurisprudence—and his lawyer, who conceived of this plea, had been none other than Edwin Stanton, now the Union secretary of war. Sickles compounded his notoriety by taking his besmirched wife back to his bosom. In 1861 he raised a brigade of New Yorkers, and by 1863 he had risen to corps command through a combination of aggressive fighting and political pull.

On July 2 Sickles felt unhappy about the exposed nature of the low ground he was ordered to defend, at the southern end of Cemetery Ridge before it thrusts upward at Little Round Top. This position was commanded by higher ground about a mile to his front, where the Emmitsburg road ran alongside a peach orchard. Sickles therefore moved his men forward in midafternoon to hold a salient, with its apex in the peach orchard and its left anchored in a maze of boulders locally called Devil's Den, just below Little Round Top. Although this position gave Sickles higher ground to defend, it left his two divisions unconnected to the rest of the Union line and vulnerable to enemy attack on both flanks. As matters turned out, it also left Little Round Top uncovered. By the time Meade learned what Sickles had done, it was too late to order him back to the original line.

AS TWO ALABAMA REGIMENTS ADVANCED ON LITTLE ROUND TOP, THE 20TH MAINE DEPLOYED BEHIND TREES, ROCKS, AND UNDERBRUSH TO MEET THE ONSLAUGHT.

Longstreet had already begun his attack.

Sickles's unwise move may have unwittingly foiled Lee's hopes. Finding the Union left in an unexpected position, Longstreet probably should have notified Lee. Scouts reported that Little Round Top and Round Top, a higher, steeper wooded hill to its south, were unoccupied. This opened the way for a flanking move around to the Union rear. Major General John Bell Hood, Longstreet's most aggressive division commander, urged a change of attack plan to take advantage of this opportunity. But Longstreet had already tried to change Lee's mind. He did not want to risk another rebuff. Lee had ordered him to attack here, and here he meant to attack. At 4:00 P.M. his brigades started forward in echelon from right to left.

During the next four hours some of the war's bloodiest fighting occurred in the peach orchard, in a wheat field east of the orchard, at Devil's Den, and on Little Round Top —place names that became forever enshrined in American memory. Longstreet's twenty thousand yelling veterans smashed through the salient with attacks that shattered Sickles's leg and crushed his undersized corps of ten thousand men. As Sickles was carried off the field on a stretcher, a rumor began to spread among his troops that he was dead. To disprove the rumor and prevent panic from spreading, Sickles lit a cigar and smoked it jauntily despite his pain. His amputated leg was preserved in formaldehyde at a medical laboratory in Washington, where in later years Sickles would occasionally visit it.

One of Longstreet's brigades, Mississippians all, captured a battery and penetrated almost to Cemetery Ridge before being driven back by the loss of half of its fifteen hundred men. One of the casualties was Brigadier General William Barksdale, a prewar Mississippi politician and fire-eating secessionist who had joined the army in a search for glory. At

★ ★ ★ ★ ★ ★

AFTER A VICIOUS FIGHT LASTING MORE THAN AN HOUR, THE 20TH MAINE WAS ALMOST OUT OF AMMUNITION AND ABOUT TO BE OVERRUN. WITH FEW OTHER OPTIONS, CHAMBERLAIN ORDERED A BAYONET CHARGE, WHICH SO SHOCKED THE EXHAUSTED CONFEDERATE ATTACKERS, THEY SURRENDERED WITHIN A FEW MINUTES.

Gettysburg he found it, leading his brigade into the thick of the action, his long white hair streaming out as he rode forward at the head of his men, his face "radiant with joy," waving his sword and shouting, "Forward, men! Forward!" before he fell, shot through the legs and chest, dying in Union hands.

The experience of Barksdale's brigade paralleled that of the rest of Longstreet's men—initial success followed by eventual repulse, with losses approaching 50 percent in some units. Skillful tactical handling of Union troops contained Confederate thrusts and held an unbroken line along Cemetery Ridge. Meade and his subordinates, especially Major General Winfield Scott Hancock of the 2nd Corps, rushed reinforcements from three Union corps to shore up the broken remnants of Sickles's corps. Brigade and regimental commanders demonstrated exceptional leadership and initiative—as well as courage.

More than any other single unit, perhaps, the 1st Minnesota Infantry earned undying fame at Gettysburg. At the height of the fighting, at about 7:00 P.M., an Alabama brigade pursuing broken remnants of Sickles's corps threatened to punch right through Cemetery Ridge about a mile north of Little Round Top. Hancock was hurrying reinforcements toward the spot, but for a critical ten minutes the only Union troops nearby were eight companies of the 1st Minnesota—262 men. Hancock immediately shouted to the regiment's colonel, "Charge those lines!"—it was 262 men against 1,500. As the Minnesota colonel told the story: "Every man realized in an instant what that order meant—death or wounds to us all; the sacrifice of the regiment to gain a few minutes time and save the position, and probably the battlefield—and every man saw and accepted the necessity for the sacrifice." With a yell, they tore into the Alabamians and gave Hancock his ten minutes—at the cost of 215 Minnesotans killed or wounded, including the colonel and all but three of his officers—a casualty rate of 82 percent, the highest of the war for any Union regiment in a single action.

At the same hour a mile to the south, another Union regiment won almost equal fame, at less cost, in a crucial action that saved the left flank of the Union line at Little Round Top. Rising above the surrounding countryside, the two Round Tops dominated the south end of Cemetery Ridge. If the Confederates got artillery up there, they could enfilade the Union line. The higher hill, Round Top, was so steep and wooded that it would have taken hours to drag guns up its rugged, rocky slope and fell trees for a line of fire. So the crucial position was Little Round Top, with its open face to the west and northwest and access via a farm path.

While the fighting in Devil's Den and the wheat field raged nearby, another brigade of Alabamians advanced to seize Little Round Top. Minutes earlier nothing but a Union signal station had stood in their way. Meade's chief of engineers, General Gouverneur K. Warren, had discovered this appalling situation as enemy troops approached. Galloping down the hill, Warren persuaded the 5th Corps commander to detach a brigade from the reinforcements heading toward the wheat field and send it double-timing to the crest of Little Round Top just in time to meet the charging Confederates.

Posted at the far left of this brigade was the 20th Maine Infantry, commanded by Colonel Joshua Lawrence Chamberlain, surely the most remarkable of the many schoolteachers and college professors who had left their classrooms to take up arms. A year before the battle of Gettysburg, he had been a professor of rhetoric and modern languages at Bowdoin College. Several of Chamberlain's ancestors had fought in the American Revolution, and his father had wanted young Lawrence (as the family called him) to pursue a military career. But his mother had wanted him to become a clergyman. She appeared to have gotten her way; Lawrence graduated Phi Beta Kappa from Bowdoin and earned a B.D. from Bangor Theological Seminary. In 1855 Cham-

"The two lines met and broke and mingled in the shock. The crush of musketry gave way to cuts and thrusts. How men held on, each one knows,—not I. But manhood commands admiration."

—Chamberlain on the climax of the fight at Little Round Top, July 2, 1863

berlain accepted a professorship at Bowdoin, succeeding Calvin Stowe, whose wife, Harriet Beecher Stowe, had written *Uncle Tom's Cabin* while Chamberlain was a student at Bowdoin. Chamberlain knew Mrs. Stowe, and, like thousands of others, he was profoundly moved by her novel to work for the abolition of slavery and the betterment of humankind.

In 1862 he got his chance. Although thirty-three years old and the father of three children, he considered it his duty to fight for Union and freedom. To dissuade him, in August 1862 Bowdoin offered him a two-year sabbatical in Europe. Chamberlain tentatively assented, but instead he went to the state capital and accepted a commission in the 20th Maine. He was not the only college professor in the Union army, but surely he was the only man in either army who could read seven foreign languages: Greek, Latin, Arabic, Hebrew, Syriac, French, and German.

As the shadows lengthened on the afternoon of July 2, Chamberlain found himself responsible for preventing the Confederates from rolling up the Union left. His orders were to "hold that ground at all hazards." He soon learned what that meant. For more than an hour, repeated assaults on the Union brigade defending Little Round Top surged back and forth, constantly moving to the right to overlap the Union left (Chamberlain's regiment) and enfilade the whole line. Chamberlain and his senior captain,

AFTER HIS REMARKABLE EXPLOITS AT GETTYSBURG, CHAMBERLAIN WENT ON TO BECOME ONE OF THE BEST—AND MOST OFTEN WOUNDED—BRIGADE AND DIVISION COMMANDERS IN THE ARMY OF THE POTOMAC.

Ellis Spear, a former student of Chamberlain's at Bowdoin, extended and bent back their line in an attempt to prevent this disaster. At one time or another, parts of five Confederate regiments assaulted Chamberlain's line, while to his right, on the west face of Little Round Top, the battle roared fiercely, killing Chamberlain's brigade commander, the commander of a reinforcing brigade, a colonel, and the Union artillery commander on the hill.

Finally, at about seven o'clock, with more than a third of his men down and the rest nearly out of ammunition, and with the enemy apparently forming for yet another attack, Chamberlain and the 20th Maine—perhaps the whole left flank of the Union army—seemed finished. As Chamberlain later wrote, at this crisis "my thought was running deep. . . . Five minutes more of such a defensive, and the last roll-call would sound for us. Desperate as the chances were, there was nothing for it but to take the offensive. I stepped to the colors. The men turned toward me. One word was enough,—'BAYONET!' It caught like fire, and swept along the ranks." With a wild yell, the survivors of this two-hour firefight—barely two hundred men—led by their multilingual fighting professor, lurched downhill in a bayonet charge against the shocked Alabamians. Exhausted by their uphill fighting following a twenty-five-mile march that day to reach the battlefield, the Southerners surrendered by scores—370 of them—to the adrenaline-charged

JEB STUART FINALLY ARRIVED AT GETTYSBURG ON THE EVENING OF JULY 2. THE COLD GREETING HE RECEIVED FROM LEE REFLECTED THE GENERAL'S DISSATISFACTION WITH STUART FOR BEING ABSENT AT THE TIME HE WAS MOST NEEDED.

down East Yankees. Little Round Top remained in Union hands; the Union left was secure.

Chamberlain went on to become one of the most extraordinary soldiers of the Civil War. He rose to command a brigade in the grueling campaign from the Wilderness to Petersburg in 1864. Leading his troops in an assault on Confederate trenches at Petersburg on June 18, 1864, he was shot through both hips, a wound that was usually mortal at that time. Ulysses S. Grant personally promoted the professor to brigadier general on the field—one of only

★ ★

(BELOW) CHECKERS, CHESS, CARD GAMES, READING, WRITING LETTERS, AND, IN SEASON, BASEBALL, OR SNOWBALL FIGHTS, PROVIDED DIVERSIONS FOR SOLDIERS WHEN NOT IN COMBAT. (RIGHT) THE GRAY ARROWS ON THE MAP INDICATE THE LINES OF CONFED- ERATE ATTACK ON THE AFTERNOON AND EVENING OF JULY 2. THE BROKEN BLUE ARROWS SHOW THE RETREAT OF SICKLES'S 3RD CORPS TO CEMETERY RIDGE FROM ITS ADVANCED SALIENT.

60

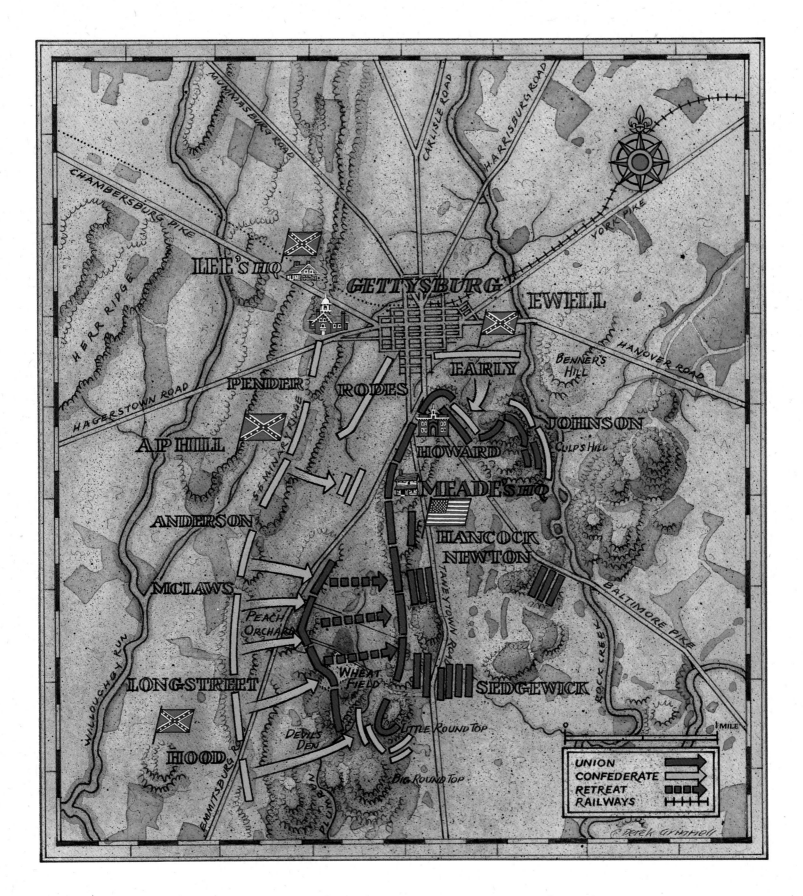

CHAMBERSBURG PIKE

MUMMASBURG ROAD

CARLISLE ROAD

HARRISBURG ROAD

YORK PIKE

HANOVER ROAD

HERR RIDGE

LEE'S HQ

GETTYSBURG

EWELL

HAGERSTOWN ROAD

PENDER

RODES

EARLY

BENNER'S HILL

AP HILL

SEMINARY RIDGE

JOHNSON

CULP'S HILL

ANDERSON

HOWARD

MEADE'S HQ

HANCOCK

NEWTON

MCLAWS

PEACH ORCHARD

WHEAT FIELD

TANEYTOWN ROAD

SEDGEWICK

ROCK CREEK

BALTIMORE PIKE

WILLOUGHBY RUN

LONGSTREET

DEVIL'S DEN

LITTLE ROUND TOP

HOOD

EMMITSBURG ROAD

PLUM RUN

BIG ROUND TOP

1 MILE

C. Derek Grinnell

UNION	
CONFEDERATE	
RETREAT	
RAILWAYS	

two such occasions in the war—so he could die at that rank. But Chamberlain beat the odds and recovered to lead his brigade—and eventually a division—in the final campaign to Appomattox.

At the battle of Quaker Road, on March 29, 1865, Chamberlain took another bullet, this one just below the heart, where it surely would have killed him had it not been deflected around his ribs by a leather case of field orders in his pocket. Chamberlain suffered only two cracked ribs and a bruised arm; he continued to lead his troops in several more fights during the next eleven days until the surrender at Appomattox. The impact of the bullet, though, had temporarily stunned him to a deathlike pallor, and for the second time several newspapers reported his

☆ ☆

THE PAINTING ON THIS AND THE FOLLOWING PAGES PORTRAYS A CRUCIAL MOMENT IN THE CAVALRY BATTLE THREE MILES EAST OF GETTYSBURG ON JULY 3. CHARGING FROM THE LEFT AT THE HEAD OF A BRIGADE OF MICHIGAN CAVALRY IS GEORGE ARMSTRONG CUSTER, RECENTLY PROMOTED FROM LIEUTENANT TO BRIGADIER GENERAL. GALLOPING TOWARD CUSTER AT FULL SPEED IS BRIGADIER GENERAL WADE HAMPTON, COMMANDER OF A CONFEDERATE CAVALRY BRIGADE, WHO WAS WOUNDED IN THE ACTION. THIS BATTLE LAUNCHED CUSTER'S RISE TO FAME, WHICH CLIMAXED AT LITTLE BIG HORN THIRTEEN YEARS LATER.

death. Chamberlain went Mark Twain one better; he twice had the pleasure of reading his own obituary. Grant selected Chamberlain to receive the Army of Northern Virginia's formal surrender of the colors at Appomattox. That was a great honor; but it is for Little Round Top that Chamberlain is mainly remembered, and for which he won the Congressional Medal of Honor.

The fighting on July 2 did not end with the charge of the 20th Maine. It continued in that sector of the field until dark. Meanwhile, the shift of Union brigades from Cemetery and Culp's hills to reinforce the units fighting

⭐ ⭐ ⭐ ⭐ ⭐ ⭐

THE MOST HONOR-ABLE—AND DANGER-OUS—POST IN A REGIMENT WAS THAT OF COLOR BEARER. BECAUSE A REGIMENT RALLIED ON THE FLAG, ENEMY SOLDIERS FOCUSED THEIR FIRE ON THE COLOR BEARER IN AN ATTEMPT TO THROW THE REGIMENT INTO CONFUSION. THE FLAG SYMBOLIZED THE CAUSE FOR WHICH THE MEN FOUGHT, AND THEY GAVE THEIR LIVES TO PROTECT IT.

Longstreet gave Ewell's corps the opportunity Lee had hoped for to convert their demonstration into an attack. But during three hours of a fruitless artillery duel with Union batteries, the opportunity slipped away.

Several of Ewell's brigades finally did advance as dusk descended. One of them seized some trenches at the base of Culp's Hill, vacated by a Federal unit sent to the other end of the battlefield, but it could advance no farther against determined opposition. Two other gray brigades scored a temporary lodgment against the hapless 11th Corps at Cemetery Hill, but a 2nd Corps brigade counterattacked in the gathering darkness and drove them back.

These actions accomplished little more than to increase the casualties. One casualty was especially poignant. Young Wesley Culp had grown up in

★ ★ ★ ★ ★ ★ ★ ★ ★ ★ ★ ★ ★ ★

ON THE MORNING OF JULY 3, LEE AND LONGSTREET DISCUSSED BATTLE PLANS FOR THE DAY. LEE OVERRULED LONGSTREET, WHO WANTED TO MANEUVER TO THE SOUTH, AND ORDERED AN ATTACK ON THE UNION CENTER. LONGSTREET'S ARTILLERY THEN MOVED INTO POSITION FOR THE BARRAGE THAT WOULD PRECEDE THE INFANTRY ATTACK.

Gettysburg. As an apprentice carriage maker he had moved to Virginia, and when war came in 1861 he enlisted—in the Confederate army. He returned with the army to Gettysburg, where on July 2 he was shot through the head and died on his uncle's farm, which had given its name to Culp's Hill.

The Confederate attacks on July 2 were uncoordinated. Lee followed his customary policy of issuing general orders but letting his corps commanders execute them in the manner they considered to be most effective. The usual skills of generalship in the Army of Northern Virginia were missing that day. On the Union side, by contrast, officers from Meade down to regimental colonels acted with initiative and coolness. They moved reinforcements to the right spots and counterattacked at the right times. As a result, when night fell the Union line remained firm except for the loss of Sickles's salient. Each side had suffered about nine thousand casualties, bringing the two-day total to nearly thirty-five thousand.

It had been the largest single-battle toll of the war thus far, but the fighting was far from over. Despite stout resistance by the Yankees, Lee believed that his indomitable veterans had achieved victory. One more push, he thought, and the enemy would break. Lee's mood and his physical condition at Gettysburg have been the subject of some controversy. He seemed unusually excited by the supposed successes of these two days. At the same time, he was perhaps weakened by a bout of diarrhea. Or maybe, as novelist Michael Shaara portrays Lee in *The Killer Angels*, a

★ ★ ★ ★ ★ ★ ★ ★ ★ ★ ★ ★ ★ ★ ★ ★ ☆

(PAGES 72–73) THE SOLDIERS IN PICKETT'S DIVISION WERE VIRGINIANS TO A MAN. THEY CAME FROM ALL WALKS OF LIFE, BUT MOST WERE FARMERS WHO HAD FLOCKED TO THE COLORS TO DEFEND THEIR STATE FROM INVASION. NOW THEY WERE THE INVADERS, NERVOUS BUT WAITING WITH STOIC COURAGE AND QUIET DETERMINATION TO GO FORWARD IN WHAT THEY KNEW WOULD BE A BLOODY ATTACK MANY OF THEM WOULD NOT SURVIVE.

flare-up of his heart condition left him by turns indecisive and belligerent, gnawed by the conviction that he had little time left.

Historians have tended to discount Shaara's interpretation. But two surgeons at the medical school of the University of Virginia, who also happen to be Civil War buffs, have recently offered evidence to support it. Lee suffered what was probably a heart attack ("myocardial infarction") at the end of March 1863. By his own account, he did not feel he had fully recovered by the summer and reported himself "more and more incapable of exertion." Piecing together Lee's own references to his health plus those of his physician, these two doctors suggest that Lee suffered from ischemic heart disease—an inadequate supply of blood to the heart—which killed him in 1870 at the age of sixty-three. "This illness," the doctors concluded in a 1992 article, may have "had a major influence on the battle of Gettysburg."

Precisely what influence is not clear. Did illness cloud Lee's judgment? Perhaps. But what might be labeled "the Chancellorsville Syndrome" was probably more important than Lee's health in this regard. Lee continued to think that he could win at Gettysburg as he had won two months earlier against greater numerical odds—by attacking. He had hit the Union flank at Chancellorsville and followed it up by a frontal attack, which worked; he intended to try the same tactics at Gettysburg. He had come to Pennsylvania in quest of a decisive victory, and he was determined not to leave without it. He believed that Meade had weakened his center to reinforce his flanks. With Pickett's fresh division, which had arrived that evening, as a spearhead, he would send three divisions against that Union center. He would also have Stuart's cavalry—which had finally turned up—circle around and come in on the Union rear, while Ewell would again assail the Union right to clamp the pincers when Pickett broke through the front. With proper coordination and leadership, his

invincible troops could not fail.

Across the way, a midnight council of Meade and his senior commanders resolved to stay and fight it out. A myth long persisted that Meade wanted to retreat but was talked out of it by his subordinates. It is true that Meade had ordered his chief of staff to draw up contingency orders for a retreat. But this was prudent generalship; Meade could have been justly criticized if he had not prepared for every contingency. Sensing the chance of victory, Meade also wanted to stand firm. Sounding almost prescient, he told Brigadier General John Gibbon, commander of a division in Hancock's 2nd Corps holding the Union center on Cemetery Ridge, that "if Lee attacks tomorrow, it will be in *your front*." Gibbon was a North Carolinian who remained loyal to the army in which he had served for twenty years, while three of his brothers went with the Confederacy. On that midnight of July 2 he gritted his teeth and told Meade that he would be ready if Lee came his way.

⭐⭐⭐⭐⭐⭐⭐⭐⭐⭐⭐⭐⭐⭐

"UP MEN, AND TO YOUR POSTS" PICKETT TOLD HIS TROOPS AS THEY PREPARED TO STEP OFF. PICKETT HAD BEEN WOUNDED A YEAR EARLIER IN THE SEVEN DAYS BATTLES, AND HE AND HIS DIVISION HAD DONE RELATIVELY LITTLE FIGHTING SINCE THEN. IN THE NEXT HOUR THEY WOULD SUFFER MORE CASUALTIES THAN IN THE REST OF THE WAR COMBINED.

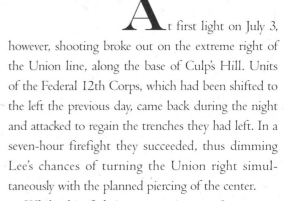

At first light on July 3, however, shooting broke out on the extreme right of the Union line, along the base of Culp's Hill. Units of the Federal 12th Corps, which had been shifted to the left the previous day, came back during the night and attacked to regain the trenches they had left. In a seven-hour firefight they succeeded, thus dimming Lee's chances of turning the Union right simultaneously with the planned piercing of the center.

While this fighting was going on, Longstreet met with Lee for a fateful discussion. "General," Longstreet said, "I have had my scouts out all night, and I find that you still have an excellent chance to move around to the left of Meade's army and maneuver him into attacking us." But Lee was no more in the mood for such a move than he had been twenty-four

(RIGHT) PESSIMISTIC
ABOUT THE CONFED-
ERATES' CHANCES
FOR SUCCESS, LONG-
STREET WATCHED
PICKETT'S MEN
ADVANCE TOWARD
UNION LINES ON
CEMETERY RIDGE
AT ABOUT 3:00 P.M.
ON JULY 3.
(OPPOSITE PAGE) TO
REACH UNION LINES
ON CEMETERY
RIDGE, CONFED-
ERATE ATTACKERS
HAD TO CROSS THE
EMMITSBURG ROAD,
APPROXIMATELY
THREE HUNDRED
YARDS FROM UNION
SOLDIERS. BOR-
DERING THE ROAD
WAS A SPLIT RAIL
FENCE BLOCKING
THE CONFEDERATES'
PATH. UNDER HEAVY
FIRE, A DETAIL OF
SOLDIERS WAS SENT
IN TO REMOVE THE
RAILS, A TASK THAT
LEFT MANY OF THEM
KILLED OR WOUNDED.

hours earlier. "The enemy is there," he said, pointing toward the Union line, and "I am going to take them where they are." He ordered Longstreet to prepare Pickett's fresh division and two of Hill's that had fought the first day—fewer than fifteen thousand men altogether—for an assault on the Union center, which Lee still assumed to be the weak point. To get there they would have to advance almost three-quarters of a mile across open fields under heavy artillery fire every step of the way to attack dug-in infantry. "General Lee," Longstreet later reported himself to have said, "I have been a soldier all my life. I have been with soldiers engaged in fights by couples, by squads, companies, regiments, divisions, and armies, and should know as well as anyone what soldiers can do. It is my opinion that no fifteen thousand men ever arrayed for battle can take that position."

Irritated by this near-insubordination, Lee replied impatiently that his army had beaten similar odds before—the implication being that Longstreet was not present at Chancellorsville and therefore did not know what he was talking about—and they could again. Longstreet was his senior corps commander, and Lee wanted him to organize the attack despite his reluctance. "My heart was heavy," Longstreet recalled.

☆ ☆ ☆ ☆ ☆ ☆ ☆ ☆ ☆ ☆ ☆ ☆ ☆ ☆ ☆ ☆ ☆ ☆ ☆

(PAGES 78–81) LEWIS ARMISTEAD, COMMANDER OF ONE OF PICKETT'S BRIGADES, HOISTED HIS HAT ON HIS SWORD TO SERVE AS A GUIDE. LIKE MANY OTHER BRIGADE COMMANDERS IN THE CIVIL WAR, ARMISTEAD BELIEVED IN LEADING FROM THE FRONT.

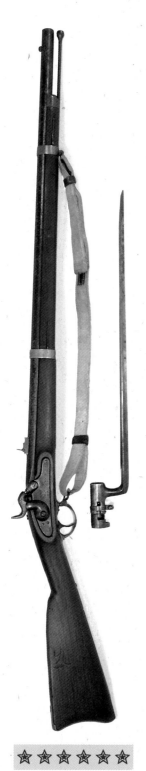

ONCE ACROSS THE FENCE, ARMISTEAD'S BRIGADE BROKE INTO A RUN UP THE GENTLE SLOPE OF CEMETERY RIDGE, THEIR FORTY-SIX-YEAR-OLD COMMANDER STILL IN THE VANGUARD.

"I could see the desperate and hopeless nature of the charge and the cruel slaughter it would cause. That day at Gettysburg was the saddest of my life."

Longstreet's account may have been colored by hindsight. In any event, he proceeded to organize an artillery barrage by 143 guns under the command of his young chief of artillery, Edward Porter Alexander, to soften up the Union defenses before the infantry went forward.

In late morning an eerie silence fell over the field as the firefight at Culp's Hill died away. At about the same time Jeb Stuart led six thousand troopers eastward from Gettysburg to circle around to the Union rear. His men and horses were still jaded from their week-long adventure, but Stuart was eager to redeem himself after the cold welcome he had received from his chief the previous day.

It was not to be. Five thousand Union horsemen barred the way. Across farm fields and pastures three miles east of Gettysburg raged a reprise of the Brandy Station cavalry battle. At the height of the clash a brigade of Michigan troops rode forward in a headlong charge against a Confederate brigade. Leading the blue horsemen was a flamboyant twenty-three-year-old brigadier, his shoulder-length red-blond ringlets streaming in the breeze. It was George Armstrong Custer, who had graduated last in his West Point class of 1861 but shown such devil-may-care charisma as a junior officer that he was jumped all the way from lieutenant to brigadier general on June 29, 1863, the youngest in the Union army, and given command of a brigade of Michigan cavalry. Opposing him at full gallop was Wade Hampton, a forty-five-year-old South Carolinian, owner of several large plantations and hundreds of slaves, who had equipped a regiment at his own expense and emerged as Stuart's senior brigadier (he would succeed Stuart when he was killed the following spring).

"Come on, you Wolverines!" yelled Custer as he spurred his horse forward. "Keep to your sabers, men, keep to your sabers!" responded Hampton from across the way. A Pennsylvania captain described the events that happened next. "As the two columns approached each other, the pace of each increased, when suddenly a crash, like the falling of timber, betokened the crisis. So sudden and violent was the collision that many of the horses were turned end over end and crushed their riders beneath them. The clashing of the sabers, the firing of pistols, the demands for surrender, and cries of combatants, filled the air." The Confederate vanguard reeled back, and Union cavalry slashed into its flank, and Stuart was stopped in his tracks. The

gray cavalry was never able to get closer than three miles from Cemetery Ridge, and a second part of Lee's plan fell through.

Meanwhile, back at Gettysburg the temporary calm was shattered by two cannon shots at 1:07 P.M. This was the signal for the Confederate barrage. Union guns replied, and for almost two hours 250 cannons filled the Pennsylvania countryside with a roar so earsplitting that, by one report, it could be heard as far away as Philadelphia. After the first few minutes, the Confederates' gun barrels heated up and the carriage trails dug into the ground, causing the gunners' aim to elevate and their

AT FREDRICKSBURG MANY UNION SOLDIERS HAD FUTILELY ATTACKED CONFEDERATES WHO WERE SHELTERED BEHIND A STONE WALL. NOW, UNION TROOPS FOUGHT FROM BEHIND A STONE WALL ON CEMETERY RIDGE.

shells to fall several hundred feet behind the Union front lines, where the infantry, lying behind stone walls, suffered little. So thick was the smoke on that hot, still day that the Confederate gunners could not see where their shots went. After an hour or so, the Union chief of artillery began to withdraw some batteries from action, to deceive the Confederates into believing they had been knocked out and to save ammunition for the infantry attack he knew was coming.

George Pickett's all-Virginia division waited with nervous impatience to go in and get the battle over with. Thirty-eight years old, Pickett had also graduated last in his West Point class. And like Custer, he wore his long hair in ringlets. With his face adorned by a drooping mustache and goatee, Pickett looked like a cross between a Cavalier dandy and a riverboat gambler.

He affected the romantic style of Sir Walter Scott. Pickett and his division had seen relatively little action since the Seven Days battles a year earlier, in which Pickett had been wounded. He was eager to win everlasting glory at Gettysburg.

Less eager, but driven by honor and pride, were Pickett's brigade commanders, all of them older than Pickett: Lewis A. Armistead, Richard B. Garnett, and James L. Kemper. Kemper was a hotheaded secessionist and political general; Armistead and Garnett were professionals with something to prove. Every generation of Virginia Armisteads since 1636 had fought in one of Britain's or America's wars; Lewis's father and four of his uncles had fought in the War of 1812. It must have been a matter of some family shame, therefore, when young Lewis was expelled from West Point in 1836, reportedly for hitting classmate Jubal Early over the head with a dinner plate. Armistead went into the army in 1839 and worked his way up to captain before resigning to join the Confederacy in 1861. One of his closest friends in the old army was Winfield Scott Hancock, who was waiting for him across the way as commander of the Union 2nd Corps, defending the sector the Confederates intended to attack.

Garnett had commanded the Stonewall Brigade, under Stonewall Jackson, in the battle of Kernstown in March 1862. When his men ran out of ammunition, he pulled them back. Jackson court-martialed him for disobedience of orders and cowardice. Garnett was never tried, and was subsequently given a

☆ ☆ ☆ ☆ ☆ ☆ ☆ ☆ ☆ ☆ ☆ ☆ ☆ ☆ ☆

ABOUT TWO HUNDRED YARDS FROM UNION LINES, THE CONFEDERATES STOPPED THEIR ADVANCE TO EXCHANGE FIRE WITH THE UNION INFANTRY. FOR MANY, IT WAS A FATAL PAUSE. UNION REGIMENTS WORKED THEIR WAY AROUND TO THE FLANKS OF PICKETT'S AND PETTIGREW'S DIVISIONS AND POURED IN DEADLY ENFILADING VOLLEYS, STOPPING WHOLE REGIMENTS IN THEIR TRACKS.

brigade under Pickett, but he felt the need to erase the stain on his honor. He was too sick to participate in this attack on foot and was determined to lead his brigade on horseback, even though that would make him the prime target of every Union rifle within range.

As Armistead and Garnett gazed across the fields to the woods on Cemetery Ridge they were ordered to assault, Garnett commented, "This is a desperate thing to attempt." "It is," agreed Armistead. "But the issue is with the Almighty, and we must leave it in his hands."

Pickett's division would go forward on the right of the Confederate line of attack. To their left would be the divisions of Isaac Trimble, a grizzled Marylander full of fire for the Confederate cause, and Johnston Pettigrew, a native of North Carolina and another fighting professor. The tension mounting, their troops waited in the woods along Seminary Ridge as Union shells and tree branches severed by shells fell on and around them. Confederate batteries were beginning to run short of ammunition shortly before three o'clock. Alexander's barrage seemed to have disabled enemy artillery, whose rate of fire had diminished. Alexander sent word to Longstreet that it was now or never for the infantry to advance. Pickett pleaded with Longstreet to give the word. Longstreet later wrote that "my feelings had so overcome me that I could not speak, for fear of betraying my want of confidence." All he could do was

HIS HAT PIERCED BY HIS SWORD, ARMISTEAD LED A FEW SCORE OF MEN THROUGH A BREACH IN THE UNION CENTER WHERE THE STONE WALL MADE A RIGHT ANGLE TOWARD THE UNION REAR. ARMISTEAD RECEIVED A MORTAL WOUND, AND NEARLY ALL THE MEN WITH HIM WERE KILLED OR CAPTURED.

nod. That was enough for Pickett. He rushed back to his men and gave them a short speech, concluding, "Up men, and to your posts! Don't forget today that you are from old Virginia."

Forth they went, line after line spread across a front nearly a mile wide. Almost as soon as they emerged from the trees, enemy artillery began to find the range, and it quickly became apparent that few if any Union cannons had really been knocked out. Amid the smoke, noise, and chaos of exploding shells, Armistead put his hat on the point of his sword and held it high as a guide. Men began to fall, but silently the ranks continued to move forward—no rebel yell this time—almost as if on the parade ground. It was an awesome spectacle that participants on both sides remembered until the end of their lives—which for many came within the next half hour.

As they approached the Union line, Pickett's division obliqued left so that the concentrated force of all three divisions focused on a front only five hun-

★ ★ ★ ★ ★ ★ ★ ★ ★ ★ ★ ★ ★ ★ ★

AS CONFEDERATE ATTACKERS LEAPED ACROSS THE STONE WALL, THEY MET UNION RESERVES RUNNING FORWARD TO FILL THE GAP. THE THINNED RANKS OF SOUTHERN REGI- MENTS ARE INDI- CATED BY THE NUMEROUS CONFED- ERATE BATTLE FLAGS, EACH REPRE- SENTING A REGIMENT FIGHTING ALONG A FRONT ONLY A FEW YARDS WIDE.

dred yards wide. Yankee artillery and infantry waited behind a stone wall—just as Confederate troops had waited at Fredericksburg seven months earlier. As the attackers crossed the Emmitsburg road less than three hundred yards from the wall, Union artillery switched to canister (bullets packed into casings), and blue riflemen sent sheets of lead into the dense lines of gray infantry. Regiments from Vermont, Ohio, and New York swung out to the left and right of the stone wall to pour a devastating fire into both Confederate flanks, which began to melt away like hail on a hot summer day.

In the center, too, all was chaos. Longstreet's worst fears were coming true. Trimble went down with a wound that would cost him a leg. Pettigrew received a flesh wound in the hand. Garnett's riderless horse bolted out of the smoke; later, his master's body was buried in a mass grave with his men and never found. Kemper was crippled by a severe wound. All thirteen of the colonels in Pickett's division were wounded.

★ ★ ★ ★ ★ ★ ★ ★ ★ ★ ★ ★ ★ ★ ★ ★

AT THE POINT OF DEEPEST CONFEDERATE PENETRATION —LOOKING SOUTH ALONG UNION LINES WHERE THE STONE WALL MAKES ITS RIGHT-ANGLE TURN—THE 26TH NORTH CAROLINA OF JOHNSTON PETTIGREW'S DIVISION (FOREGROUND) IS STOPPED SHORT OF THE WALL, WHILE PICKETT'S VIRGINIANS ARE CUT DOWN WHILE FIGHTING INSIDE THE ANGLE (BACKGROUND).

Several hundred men with Armistead broke through the line at an angle to the stone wall, only to be killed or captured; Armistead received a mortal wound as he placed his hand on an enemy cannon to claim its capture. By four o'clock it was all over. Unwounded but dazed Confederate survivors stumbled back to their starting point. Barely half returned; in Pickett's division only two-fifths came back.

As the men reached their own lines they found Lee and Longstreet working feverishly to establish a defense against an expected Union counterattack. "General Pickett," said Lee to a slumped figure from whom all thoughts of glory had fled, "place your division in the rear of this hill, and be ready to repel the advance of the enemy should they follow up their advantage." "General Lee," replied Pickett in tears, "I have no division now." Lee rode among the men to buck up their spirits. "It's all my fault," he told them. "It is I who have lost this fight, and you must help me out of it the best way you can. All good men must rally."

Rally they did—after a fashion. But Meade did not counterattack. It was not for lack of urging by at least some of his subordinates, including Hancock. Wounded at the height of the action by a bullet that drove a bent nail from his saddle into his thigh, Hancock—misunderstanding the source of the nail—said, "They must be hard up for ammunition if they throw such a shot as that."

Meade's failure to follow up his great victory with a vigorous counterthrust provoked criticism at the time and through the years. But this criticism has in turn elicited defense of his decision. A heavy load of responsibility rested on Meade's shoulders. He had been in command of the army for only six days. For three of them the army had been fighting for the nation's life, from Meade's perspective, and had narrowly saved it. Meade could not yet have known how badly the enemy was hurt—at least twenty-five thou-

★★★★★★

UNION TROOPS
IMMEDIATELY
COUNTERATTACKED
AFTER ARMISTEAD
MADE A TEMPORARY
BREAK-THROUGH AT
THE WALL.

"Place your division in the rear of the hill."

"General Lee, I have no division now.
Armistead is down, Garnett is down, and
Kemper is mortally wounded."

— Lee to Pickett after repulse of Pickett's charge

sand killed, wounded, and captured, one-third of Lee's army—or that their artillery ammunition was so low. He did know that his own army had been badly hurt—twenty-three thousand casualties, one-fourth of the total Union strength at Gettysburg.

Meade's lack of aggressiveness was also caused by his respect for the enemy. He could scarcely believe that he had beaten the victors of Chancellorsville. Meade later explained that he had not wanted to

©MKünstler '93

⭐ ⭐ ⭐ ⭐ ⭐ ⭐

BARELY HALF OF
THE THIRTEEN
THOUSAND CONFED-
ERATE ATTACKERS
MADE IT BACK TO
THEIR OWN LINES,
INCLUDING MANY
WALKING WOUNDED
WHO WERE ASSISTED
BY THEIR COMRADES.

follow "the bad example [Lee] had set me, in ruining himself attacking a strong position."

"We have done well enough," he said to a cavalry officer eager to do more. Some other officers felt the same way; one of them commented that "the glorious success of the Army of the Potomac has electrified all. I did not believe the enemy could be whipped."

In the waning afternoon of July 3 a few units from the Federal 5th and 6th Corps advanced over the scene of the previous day's carnage in Devil's Den and the wheat field. They flushed out the rear guard of Confederates in that sector, who were pulling back to a new line. Meade apparently did have some idea of attacking in this vicinity the next day—the Fourth of July—but a heavy rain, which began about noon, soon halted the move.

The rain made even more bleak and difficult the retreat toward Virginia that Lee now considered to

be imperative. An ambulance train that was several miles long jolted over rutted roads axle-deep in mud, causing great agony for the ten thousand wounded the Army of Northern Virginia managed to take with it.

Left behind were almost seven thousand wounded to be treated by Union surgeons. Gettysburg became a vast hospital and graveyard. In all, some five thousand Union soldiers and six thousand Confederates were killed or mortally wounded there. Most of them were buried on the battlefield.

Buried also were the Confederacy's hopes for victory and the South's quest for independence. The Fourth of July 1863 was an ironic or a glorious holiday—depending on one's viewpoint. For on that day not only did Lee begin the weary and painful retreat to Virginia: Vicksburg also surrendered to Grant. It was the biggest turning point of the war.

THE MAP (RIGHT) SHOWS THE ACTION ON JULY 3. GRAY ARROWS INDICATE THE ROUTE OF PICKETT'S ASSAULT. THE ARROWS AND BROKEN LINES IN THE LOWER LEFT REPRESENT THE UNSUCCESSFUL UNION CAVALRY ATTACK AGAINST THE CONFEDERATE FLANK AFTER PICKETT'S CHARGE. THE MAP ON PAGES 104-05 SHOWS THE ACTION ON ALL THREE DAYS. GRAY ARROWS INDICATE CONFEDERATE ATTACKS; BLUE AND RED ARROWS INDICATE UNION RETREATS.

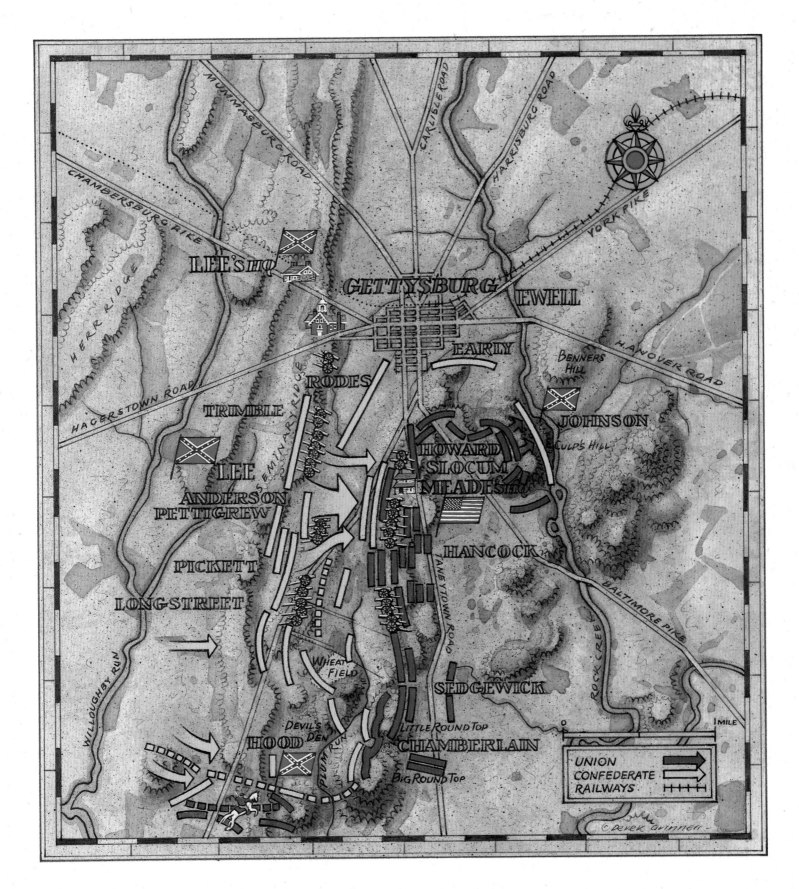

MUMMASBURG ROAD
CARLISLE ROAD
HARRISBURG ROAD
CHAMBERSBURG PIKE
YORK PIKE
HERR RIDGE
LEE'S HQ
GETTYSBURG
EWELL
HANOVER ROAD
EARLY
BENNERS HILL
HAGERSTOWN ROAD
RODES
JOHNSON
TRIMBLE
CULP'S HILL
LEE
HOWARD
SEMINARY RIDGE
SLOCUM
ANDERSON
MEADE'S HQ
PETTIGREW
PICKETT
HANCOCK
LONGSTREET
TANEYTOWN ROAD
BALTIMORE PIKE
WILLOUGHBY RUN
WHEAT FIELD
SEDGEWICK
ROCK CREEK
1 MILE
DEVIL'S DEN
LITTLE ROUND TOP
HOOD
PLUM RUN
CHAMBERLAIN
BIG ROUND TOP
UNION
CONFEDERATE
RAILWAYS

© Derek Grinnell

103

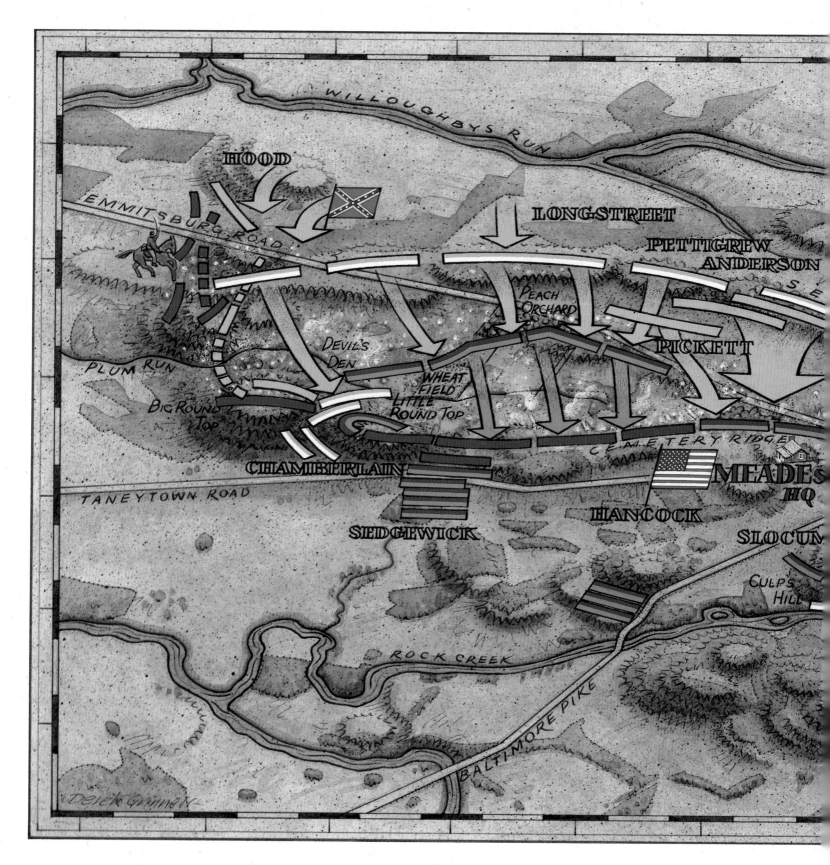

WILLOUGHBYS RUN

HOOD

EMMITSBURG ROAD

LONGSTREET

PETTIGREW
ANDERSON

PEACH
ORCHARD

PLUM RUN

DEVIL'S
DEN

WHEAT
FIELD

PICKETT

BIG ROUND
TOP

LITTLE
ROUND TOP

CEMETERY RIDGE

CHAMBERLAIN

MEADES
HQ

TANEYTOWN ROAD

SEDGEWICK

HANCOCK

SLOCUM

CULPS
HILL

ROCK CREEK

BALTIMORE PIKE

Derek Grinnell

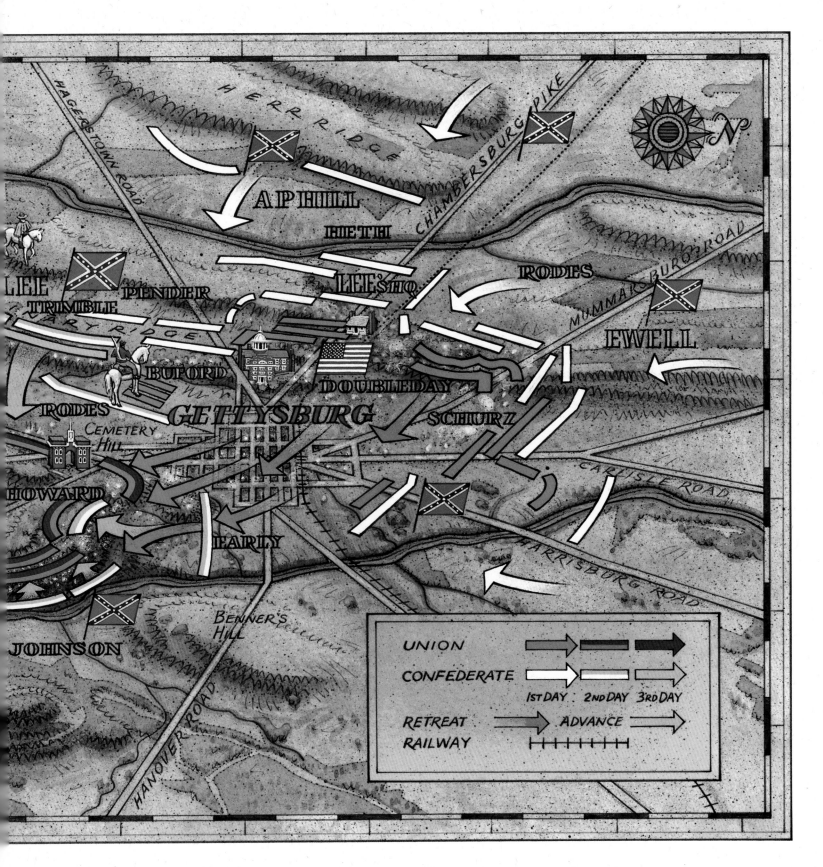

HAGERSTOWN ROAD

HERR RIDGE

CHAMBERSBURG PIKE

A P HILL

HETH

MUMMASBURG ROAD

RODES

LEE

TRIMBLE

PENDER

SEMINARY RIDGE

LEE'S HQ

RODES

EWELL

BUFORD

DOUBLEDAY

RODES

GETTYSBURG

SCHURZ

CEMETERY HILL

CARLISLE ROAD

HOWARD

EARLY

HARRISBURG ROAD

BENNER'S HILL

JOHNSON

N

UNION			
CONFEDERATE			
	1ST DAY	2ND DAY	3RD DAY
RETREAT		ADVANCE	
RAILWAY			

HANOVER ROAD

A NEW BIRTH OF FREEDOM

E PLURIBUS UNUM

PART · THREE

GENERAL MEADE'S OPPORTU-

NITY TO INFLICT AN EVEN GREATER BLOW TO CONFEDERATE HOPES

DID NOT END WITH LEE'S RETREAT FROM GETTYSBURG. IN FACT,

THE RETREAT PROVIDED NEW CHANCES TO CUT OFF AND CAPTURE

PART OF THE CRIPPLED ARMY OF NORTHERN VIRGINIA. SEVERAL

DAYS OF RAIN TURNED ROADS INTO QUAGMIRES, WHICH SLOWED

BOTH CONFEDERATE PROGRESS AND UNION PURSUIT. BUT NORTH-

ERN CAVALRY DESTROYED THE CONFEDERATE PONTOON BRIDGE

OVER THE POTOMAC, AND THE RAIN MADE ALL FORDS OVER THE

AS THE DAZED SURVIVORS OF PICKETT'S CHARGE STUMBLED BACK TO THEIR OWN LINES ON THE SULTRY AFTERNOON OF JULY 3, THEY ENCOUNTERED GENERAL LEE HIMSELF RIDING AMONG THEM TO RALLY THEIR SPIRITS. "IT'S ALL MY FAULT," HE SAID. "IT IS I WHO HAVE LOST THIS FIGHT, AND YOU MUST HELP ME OUT OF IT IN THE BEST WAY YOU CAN."

107

river impassable. The Confederates were trapped north of the Potomac for several days while Lee's engineer corps frantically tore down buildings to construct a new set of pontoons. Lee fortified a defensive perimeter at Williamsport, Maryland, with both flanks on the river and waited for the Yankees to attack.

Lincoln wanted Meade to do just that. "If General Meade can complete his work by the literal or substantial destruction of Lee's army," said the Union president on July 7, "the rebellion will be over." From General in Chief Henry W. Halleck in Washington came telegrams to ordering Meade to "push forward, and fight Lee before he can cross the Potomac." Lincoln hovered around the War Department telegraph office "anxious and impatient" for news that Meade was doing so. But the Union commander and his men were exhausted from lack of sleep and endless slogging through bottomless mud. The Confederate earthworks at Williamsport were formidable, even though Lee had only forty-five thousand tired troops to defend them, while reinforcements had brought Meade's strength back up to eighty-five thousand. Meade's famous temper grew short as messages from Halleck bombarded him. Lincoln's temper also grew short. When Meade finally telegraphed on July 12 that he intended "to attack them tomorrow, unless something intervenes," Lincoln commented acidly: "They will be ready to fight a magnificent battle when there is no enemy there to fight."

Events proved Lincoln right. A pretended deserter (a favorite Confederate ruse) had entered Union lines near Williamsport and reported that the Army of Northern Virginia was in fine fettle, eager for another fight. This news intensified Meade's reluctance to follow Lee's example "in ruining himself attacking a strong position." He allowed his corps commanders to talk him out of attacking on the 13th. When the Army of the Potomac finally moved forward on July 14, the soldiers found nothing but a

rear guard. The slippery rebels had vanished across a patched-together bridge during the night. "Great God!" exclaimed Lincoln when he heard this news. "What does it mean? We had them in our grasp. We had only to stretch forth our hands and they were ours. Our Army held the war in the hollow of their hand and they would not close it."

Lincoln's estimate of the situation at Williamsport may not have been accurate. An assault on the Confederate works might have succeeded—with heavy Union casualties—or it might not have. In either case, the destruction of Lee's veteran army was scarcely a sure thing. When word of Lincoln's dissatisfaction reached Meade, the testy general offered his resignation. This was a serious matter. Despite his slowness and caution, Meade had won great public acclaim for the victory at Gettysburg. Lincoln could hardly afford to sack him two weeks after the battle. So he refused to accept the resignation, and sat down to write Meade a soothing letter.

After a good start, however, the letter did not come across as very soothing. "My dear General," wrote Lincoln, "I am very—very—grateful to you for the magnificent success you gave the cause of the country at Gettysburg." But, the president went on as he warmed to the subject, "I do not believe you appreciate the magnitude of the misfortune involved in Lee's escape. He was within your easy grasp, and to have closed upon him would, in connection with our other late successes, have ended the war. As it is, the war will be prolonged indefinitely. Your golden opportunity is gone, and I am distressed immeasurably because of it." Upon reflection, as he reread his letter, Lincoln concluded that it was unlikely to mollify Meade's feelings, so he never sent it.

Lincoln's temper soon abated. By early August his private secretary wrote that the president "is in fine whack. I have seldom seen him so serene." In large part this was because of the "other late successes" he had referred to in his unsent letter to Meade. These successes included not only the capture of Vicksburg but

THE FATIGUE AND DEPRESSION OF THE ARMY OF NORTHERN VIRGINIA ON ITS RETREAT AFTER GETTYSBURG WERE COMPOUNDED BY HEAVY RAINS THAT TURNED DIRT ROADS INTO BOTTOMLESS MUD. IN THIS CRISIS, LEE DEPENDED MORE THAN EVER ON THE STEADY NERVES OF HIS "OLD WAR-HORSE," GENERAL JAMES LONGSTREET.

also of Port Hudson, two hundred miles to the south, which together brought the whole Mississippi River under Union control and split the Confederacy in two. "The Father of Waters again goes unvexed to the sea," pronounced Lincoln.

In Tennessee, Union forces had won an almost bloodless victory simultaneously with the battle of Gettysburg and the capture of Vicksburg. With speed and stealth, the Union Army of the Cumberland had struck through passes in the Cumberland foothills and forced Braxton Bragg's Army of Tennessee to retreat all the way to Chattanooga.

These were strategic accomplishments of great import. But in the public mind, in both the North and South, they paled in comparison with the battle of Gettysburg. The "media" had always focused most of their attention on the eastern theater, with its titanic clashes between the Army of the Potomac and the Army of

Northern Virginia. Headlines in Northern newspapers testified to this emphasis. "VICTORY! WATERLOO ECLIPSED!" blazoned a Philadelphia newspaper in a story about Gettysburg. The glad tidings reached Washington the day after Pickett's repulse, making this the capital's most glorious Fourth of July ever. "I never knew such excitement in Washington," wrote one observer.

When word arrived three days later of the surrender at Vicksburg, the excitement doubled. Lincoln appeared that day on a White House balcony to tell a crowd of serenaders that the "gigantic Rebellion," whose purpose was to "overthrow the principle that all men are created equal," had been dealt a crippling blow.

In New York City a lawyer wrote in his diary when he heard the news of Gettysburg that "the results of this victory are priceless. The charm of Robert Lee's invincibility is broken. The Army of the Potomac has at last found a general that can handle it, and has

stood nobly up to its terrible work in spite of its long disheartening list of hard-fought failures. Copperheads are palsied and dumb for the moment at least. Government is strengthened four-fold at home and abroad."

The final sentence was truer than the diarist could know. Confederate Vice-President Alexander Stephens was on his way under flag of truce to Union lines at Norfolk as the battle of Gettysburg reached its climax. Jefferson Davis had hoped that Stephens might reach Washington from the south while Lee's victorious army was marching toward it from the north. Reports of Stephens's mission and of Gettysburg's outcome reached the White House at the same time. Lincoln thereupon sent a curt refusal to Stephens's request for a pass through the lines.

In London the news of Gettysburg and Vicksburg drove the final nail into the coffin of Confederate hopes for recognition. "The disaster of the rebels are unredeemed by even any hope of success," wrote young Henry Adams from London, where he was secretary to his father, the American minister to the Court of St. James. "It is now conceded that all idea of [British] intervention is at an end."

Southern gloom mirrored Northern gladness. "The news from Lee's army is appalling," wrote a Confederate War Department clerk, John Jones, in his diary on July 9. "This is the darkest day of the war." The fire-eating Virginia secessionist Edmund Ruffin wrote that he "never before felt so despondent as to our struggle." A Confederate soldier who had fought at Gettysburg wrote afterward to his sister: "We got a bad whiping. They are awhiping us at every point. I hope they would make peace so that we that is alive yet would get home agane." Desertion rates rose sharply in the Army of Northern Virginia. Unprecedented criticisms of Lee crept into Southern newspaper accounts of Gettysburg.

Depressed by all this and by his lack of robust health, Lee wrote a startling letter to President Davis on August 8. "The general remedy for the want of

★ ★ ★ ★ ★ ★

THE CONFEDERATE ARMY HAD AN ENORMOUS MANPOWER LOSS IN PRISONERS TAKEN AT GETTYSBURG. FIVE THOUSAND UNWOUNDED SOLDIERS SURRENDERED TO UNION FORCES, MORE THAN HALF OF THEM DURING THE REPULSE OF PICKETT'S CHARGE. IN ADDITION, NEARLY SEVEN THOUSAND WOUNDED CONFEDERATES WERE LEFT BEHIND AS PRISONERS, TO BE CARED FOR BY UNION MEDICAL PERSONNEL.

success in a military commander is his removal," said the general to his commander in chief. "I have seen and heard of expressions of discontent in the public journals as the result of the expedition. . . . I cannot even accomplish what I myself desire. How can I fulfill the expectations of others? . . . Everything, therefore, points to the advantages to be derived from a new commander. . . . I, therefore, in all sincerity, request Your Excellency to take measures to supply my place."

This from a general whose stunning achievements during the year before Gettysburg had won the admiration of the Western world. Of course, Davis refused to accept Lee's resignation. "To ask me to substitute for you someone in my judgment more fit to command," the president wrote to Lee, "is to demand an impossibility."

But spirits remained low in Richmond. "We are now in the darkest hour of our political existence," said Davis to an associate. And Ordnance Chief Josiah Gorgas, who had performed miracles in keeping Confederate forces supplied with arms and ammunition, wrote in his diary at the end of July 1863: "Events have succeeded one another with disastrous rapidity. One brief month ago we were apparently at the point of success. Lee was in Pennsylvania, threatening Harrisburgh, and even Philadelphia. Vicksburgh seemed to laugh all Grant's efforts to scorn. . . . Port Hudson had beaten off Banks' force. . . . It seems incredible that human power could effect such a change in so brief a space. Yesterday we rode on the pinnacle of success—today absolute ruin seems to be our portion. The Confederacy totters to its destruction."

Predictions of imminent demise proved premature. As Lincoln had lamented in his unsent letter to Meade, "The war will be prolonged indefinitely." Nevertheless, the months after Gettysburg brought a marked rise in Northerners' morale. One important consequence was a vastly more positive attitude toward emancipation. Gone was the carping criticism of the policy from within the Union army. Even Democratic newspapers and politicians soft-pedaled their opposition—for the time being.

Simultaneous events in New York City and South Carolina two weeks after Gettysburg accelerated and dramatized this shift in opinion. In New York, working-class whites, who were the backbone of anti-emancipation and Democratic strength, erupted in several days of rioting against conscription, which they believed would require them to fight in the army for the freedom of "niggers," who were the particular targets of the rioters' hatred. At the same time, on July 18, the 54th Massachusetts Infantry, one of the first black regiments organized in the Union army, spearheaded a bloody assault on Fort Wagner, part of the Confederate defenses of Charleston. Fighting with great courage, the 54th lost nearly half its men in the attack.

These dual events eight hundred miles apart prompted a massive shift in Northern opinion toward a conviction that black men who fought for the Union were more deserving of rights and respect than white men who rioted against it. President Lincoln put it best. Addressing the foes of emancipation in a public letter dated August 26, 1863, Lincoln said that when victory was finally achieved in the war, "there will be some black men who can remember that, with silver tongue, and clenched teeth, and steady eye, and well-poised bayonet, they have helped mankind on to this great consummation; while, I fear, there will be some white ones, unable to forget that, with malignant heart, and deceitful speech, they have strove to hinder it."

The upbeat mood of the Northern electorate manifested itself in several important off-year state elections in the fall of 1863. Republicans won decisive victories everywhere. They interpreted them as a mandate for their emancipation policy as well as for the cause of Union. If the Emancipation Proclamation had been submitted to a referendum a year earlier, commented an Illinois newspaper, "there is little

THE AVERAGE AGE OF CIVIL WAR SOLDIERS AT THE TIME OF THEIR ENLISTMENT WAS TWENTY-FOUR. BUT THOUSANDS OF BOYS AGED SEVENTEEN AND EVEN YOUNGER LIED ABOUT THEIR AGE AND BECAME COMBAT SOLDIERS, LIKE THESE YOUNG UNION VETERANS OF THE WAR'S BLOODIEST BATTLE.

THE ARMY OF NORTHERN VIRGINIA CARRIED AT LEAST TEN THOUSAND WOUNDED MEN BACK TOWARD VIRGINIA IN EVERY KIND OF VEHICLE, FROM ARMY AMBULANCES TO COMMANDEERED FARM WAGONS. THE WOUNDED SUFFERED ADDITIONAL AGONIES FROM THE ROUGH, RUTTED ROADS; MANY DIED ON THE WAY.

doubt that the voice of a majority would have been against it. And not a year has passed before it is approved by an overwhelming majority." A New York diarist noted that "the change of opinion on this slavery question since 1860 is a great historical fact. God pardon our blindness of three years ago."

No single event did more to change the mood in the North than the victory at Gettysburg. It was appropriate, therefore, that Lincoln should offer his most profound and eloquent statement there on the meaning of this new birth of freedom. Soon after the battle, a local lawyer had proposed to the governor of Pennsylvania the establishment of a soldiers' cemetery, where the Union dead, now buried in hundreds of shallow mass graves around the battlefield, could be reinterred with dignity and honor. The governor contacted the governors of other Northern states whose soldiers had died at Gettysburg, and the project went forward. (It became the model for reinterment of Union war dead in two dozen national cemeteries after the war; many Confederate dead were also reburied in Confederate cemeteries throughout the South.) The dedication of the soldiers' cemetery, adjacent to the local burial ground on Cemetery Hill where some of the fighting had occurred, took place on November 19, 1863.

The main speaker at the dedication, Edward Everett, was the foremost orator in the United States. His two-hour oration did not disappoint the throng of fifteen thousand gathered for the ceremony on that fine autumn day. But it was the "few appropriate remarks" by Lincoln that became the classic expression of the meaning of Gettysburg. Everett recognized this; the next day he penned a gracious note to Lincoln: "I should flatter myself, that I came as near to the central idea of the occasion, in two hours, as you did in two minutes."

The Gettysburg Address

Four score and seven years ago our fathers brought forth on this continent,
a new nation, conceived in Liberty, and dedicated to the proposition
that all men are created equal.

Now we are engaged in a great civil war, testing whether that nation,
or any nation so conceived and so dedicated, can long endure. We are met on
a great battlefield of that war. We have come to dedicate a portion of that field,
as a final resting place for those who here gave their lives that that nation might live.

It is altogether fitting and proper that we should do this.

But, in a larger sense, we can not dedicate—we can not consecrate—
we can not hallow—this ground. The brave men, living and dead,
who struggled here, have consecrated it, far above our poor power to add or detract.

The world will little note, nor long remember what we say here, but it can
never forget what they did here. It is for us the living, rather, to be dedicated here
to the unfinished work which they who fought here have thus far so nobly advanced.

It is rather for us to be here dedicated to the great task remaining before us—
that from these honored dead we take increased devotion to that cause
for which they gave the last full measure of devotion—that we here highly resolve
that these dead shall not have died in vain—that this nation, under God,
shall have a new birth of freedom—and that government of the people,
by the people, for the people, shall not perish from the earth.

President Abraham Lincoln, November 19, 1863

117

Paintings

LEE'S "OLD WAR HORSE" (PAGES 2-3, 68-69)
GENS. LONGSTREET AND LEE, GETTYSBURG, JULY 3, 1863
1993, OPAQUE WATERCOLOR
16 1/2" x 27"
HAMMER GALLERIES, NEW YORK CITY

THE HIGH WATER MARK (PAGES 5, 8, 96-97)
GETTYSBURG, JULY 3, 1863
1988, OIL ON CANVAS
34" x 56"
MR. AND MRS. HAROLD BERNSTEIN

"WE STILL LOVE YOU, GENERAL LEE" (PAGE 7)
APPOMATTOX, VIRGINIA, APRIL 9, 1865
1992, OIL ON CANVAS
54" x 88"
HAMMER GALLERIES, NEW YORK CITY

"OH, I WISH HE WAS OURS!" (PAGES 10-11)
HAGERSTOWN, MARYLAND, JUNE 26, 1863
1991, OIL ON CANVAS
24" x 32"
MR. AND MRS. FRANK B. GILBRETH

THE EMANCIPATION PROCLAMATION (PAGE 12)
1987, OIL ON CANVAS
30" x 30"
MR. AND MRS. MICHAEL L. SHARPE

THE VIRGINIA GENTLEMAN (PAGE 14)
GEN. LEE
1993, MIXED MEDIA
16" x 10"
HAMMER GALLERIES, NEW YORK CITY

GEN. ROBERT E. LEE (PAGE 15)
1991, OIL ON BOARD
10" x 11 1/2"
HAMMER GALLERIES, NEW YORK CITY

"THE ENEMY IS THERE!" (PAGE 16)
GEN. LEE AND STAFF, GETTYSBURG
1993, OPAQUE WATERCOLOR
17" x 13 5/8"
HAMMER GALLERIES, NEW YORK CITY

GEN. JAMES LONGSTREET (PAGE 18)
SOUTH CAROLINA
1990, OIL ON BOARD
10" x 11 1/4"
HAMMER GALLERIES, NEW YORK CITY

"OLD PETE" (PAGE 19)
GEN. LONGSTREET
1993, MIXED MEDIA
14 1/4" x 9 1/2"
HAMMER GALLERIES, NEW YORK CITY

LONGSTREET AT GETTYSBURG (PAGE 21)
GEN. LONGSTREET AND STAFF
1993, OPAQUE WATERCOLOR
16 1/4" x 13"
HAMMER GALLERIES, NEW YORK CITY

THE GUNS OF GETTYSBURG (PAGE 22)
1993, MIXED MEDIA
14" x 12"
HAMMER GALLERIES, NEW YORK CITY

THE ROAD TO GETTYSBURG (PAGE 25)
1993, MIXED MEDIA
10" x 16"
HAMMER GALLERIES, NEW YORK CITY

"STRIKE UP A LIVELY AIR..." (PAGES 26-27)
CASHTOWN, PENNSYLVANIA, JULY 1, 1863
1993, MIXED MEDIA
11 1/4" x 19 1/2"
HAMMER GALLERIES, NEW YORK CITY

GEN. JOHN BUFORD (PAGE 28)
1992, OIL ON BOARD
9 5/8" x 11"
HAMMER GALLERIES, NEW YORK CITY

THE EVE OF BATTLE (PAGE 29)
GEN. BUFORD, GETTYSBURG, JUNE 30, 1863
1993, OPAQUE WATERCOLOR
13 1/4" x 11 1/8"
HAMMER GALLERIES, NEW YORK CITY

MORNING RIDERS (PAGES 30-31)
GEN. BUFORD, GETTYSBURG, JULY 3, 1863, 5:15 A.M.
1993, OPAQUE WATERCOLOR
18 1/4" x 29 5/8"
HAMMER GALLERIES, NEW YORK CITY

"Hold at All Cost" (pages 32-35)
Gen. Buford, Gettysburg, July 1, 1863
1993, Opaque watercolor
12 1/2" x 36 7/8"
Hammer Galleries, New York City

Gen. Reynolds and Staff (page 36)
Gettysburg, July 1, 1863
1993, Mixed media
8 5/8" x 15 1/8"
Hammer Galleries, New York City

Guns to the West (page 37)
Gen. Buford at the Seminary, July 1, 1863
1993, Mixed media
15" x 9 1/2"
Hammer Galleries, New York City

"There's the Devil to Pay" (pages 38-39)
Gen. Buford at Gettysburg, July 1, 1863
1990, Oil on canvas
30" x 54"
U.S. Army War College, Carlisle, Pennsylvania

Dilger at Gettysburg (pages 40-41)
July 1, 1863
1989, Oil on canvas
28" x 42"
Mr. Pat Kilbane

General J. L. Chamberlain (page 42)
Maine
1992, Oil on board
9 5/8" x 10 7/8"
Hammer Galleries, New York City

Chamberlain and the 20th Maine (page 43)
1993, Opaque watercolor
16" x 13 3/4"
Hammer Galleries, New York City

Twilight in Gettysburg (pages 44-45)
Gen. Lee, July 1, 1863
1993, Opaque watercolor
16 3/8" x 27 1/2"
Hammer Galleries, New York City

Drummer Boy (page 47)
1993, Mixed media
15" x 10"
Hammer Galleries, New York City

Gen. William Barksdale (page 48)
Mississippi
1990, Oil on board
10" x 11 1/2"

"The Grandest Charge Ever Seen" (pages 48-49)
Barksdale's Mississippians at Gettysburg,
July 2, 1863
1990, Oil on canvas
26" x 48"
Hammer Galleries, New York City

Rush to the Summit (pages 50-51)
Little Round Top, July 2, 1863
1993, Mixed media
11 5/8" x 19 1/4"
Hammer Galleries, New York City

"Fix Bayonets!" (pages 52-53)
Gen. Chamberlain, Little Round Top, July 2, 1863
1993, Mixed media
12 7/8" x 19 1/8"
Hammer Galleries, New York City

Hand to Hand (page 54)
Little Round Top, July 2, 1863
1993, Mixed media
11 1/2" x 15 1/2"
Hammer Galleries, New York City

Chamberlain's Charge (page 57)
Gettysburg, July 2, 1863
1993, Opaque watercolor
13 1/4" x 10 1/2"
Hammer Galleries, New York City

Gen. J.E.B. Stuart (page 58)
Virginia
1991, Oil on board
10" x 11 1/2"
Hammer Galleries, New York City

The Return of Stuart (pages 58-59)
Gens. Lee and Stuart, Gettysburg, July 2, 1863
1993, Opaque watercolor
13 3/8" x 17 1/2"
Hammer Galleries, New York City

A SOLDIER'S GAME (PAGE 60)
1993, MIXED MEDIA
9 7/8" x 11 3/8"
HAMMER GALLERIES, NEW YORK CITY

"GUIDES CENTER—MARCH!" (PAGES 76-77)
GEN. GARNETT, PICKETT'S CHARGE, JULY 3, 1863
1993, MIXED MEDIA
13 3/8" x 18 3/4"
HAMMER GALLERIES, NEW YORK CITY

"TO THE WALL!" (PAGES 84-85)
GEN. ARMISTEAD, PICKETT'S CHARGE, JULY 3, 1863
1993, MIXED MEDIA
10 7/8" x 19 3/8"
HAMMER GALLERIES, NEW YORK CITY

"KEEP TO YOUR SABERS, MEN!" (PAGES 62-67)
GENS. CUSTER AND HAMPTON, GETTYSBURG,
JULY 3, 1863
1992, OIL ON CANVAS
24" x 60"
HAMMER GALLERIES, NEW YORK CITY

PICKETT'S SALUTE (PAGE 70)
GETTYSBURG, JULY 3, 1863
1993, MIXED MEDIA
10 1/4" x 9 1/2"
HAMMER GALLERIES, NEW YORK CITY

"STEADY BOYS, STEADY!" (PAGES 78-81)
GEN. ARMISTEAD, PICKETT'S CHARGE, JULY 3, 1863
1993, OPAQUE WATERCOLOR
14" x 37 1/2"
HAMMER GALLERIES, NEW YORK CITY

"FASTER, MEN, FASTER!" (PAGES 86-87)
GEN. ARMISTEAD, PICKETT'S CHARGE, JULY 3, 1863
1993, MIXED MEDIA
12 3/4" x 19 1/2"
HAMMER GALLERIES, NEW YORK CITY

"WE ALL DO OUR DUTY" (PAGE 82)
GEN. LONGSTREET
1993, MIXED MEDIA
11 1/4" x 9 1/2"
HAMMER GALLERIES, NEW YORK CITY

THE COPSE OF TREES (PAGES 88-89)
GETTYSBURG, JULY 3, 1863
1993, MIXED MEDIA
13" x 19"
HAMMER GALLERIES, NEW YORK CITY

MEN OF VALOR (PAGES 72-73)
1993, OPAQUE WATERCOLOR
15 1/2" x 27 1/2"
HAMMER GALLERIES, NEW YORK CITY

THE FENCE (PAGE 83)
PICKETT'S CHARGE, JULY 3, 1863
1993, MIXED MEDIA
13 1/4" x 17 7/8"
HAMMER GALLERIES, NEW YORK CITY

VIRGINIA'S HONORED SONS (PAGES 74-75)
GEN. PICKETT, GETTYSBURG, JULY 3, 1863
1993, MIXED MEDIA
11 1/2" x 19"
HAMMER GALLERIES, NEW YORK CITY

"TRY THEM WITH THE BAYONET!" (PAGES 90-91)
PICKETT'S CHARGE, JULY 3, 1863
1993, MIXED MEDIA
12" x 19 1/2"
HAMMER GALLERIES, NEW YORK CITY

"FOLLOW ME!" (PAGES 92-93)
GEN. ARMISTEAD, PICKETT'S CHARGE, JULY 3, 1863
1993, MIXED MEDIA
11 3/8″ x 19 1/2″
HAMMER GALLERIES, NEW YORK CITY

THE WRECKAGE OF WAR (PAGE 102)
GETTYSBURG, JULY 3, 1863
1993, MIXED MEDIA
13″ x 14″
HAMMER GALLERIES, NEW YORK CITY

VETERANS OF GETTYSBURG (PAGES 112-13)
1982, OIL ON CANVAS
16″ x 20″
MR. THOMAS HUFF

THE HIGH TIDE (COVER, PAGES 94-95)
GETTYSBURG, JULY 3, 1863
1993, OPAQUE WATERCOLOR
16″ x 28 3/4″
HAMMER GALLERIES, NEW YORK CITY

"IT'S ALL MY FAULT" (PAGES 106-7)
GEN. LEE, GETTYSBURG, JULY 3, 1863
1989, OIL ON CANVAS
26″ x 48″
MR. THORNE DONNELLY, JR.

THE LONG ROAD SOUTH (PAGES 114-115)
FAIRFIELD, PENNSYLVANIA, JULY 4, 1863
1993, OPAQUE WATERCOLOR
11 7/8″ x 17 7/8″
HAMMER GALLERIES, NEW YORK CITY

THE ANGLE (PAGES 98-99)
GETTYSBURG, JULY 3, 1863
1988, OIL ON CANVAS
18″ x 24″
MR. AND MRS. MICHAEL L. SHARPE

STORM OVER GETTYSBURG (PAGE 108)
GENS. LEE AND LONGSTREET, GETTYSBURG, JULY 3, 1863
1993, OPAQUE WATERCOLOR
14 1/2″ x 12 1/2″
HAMMER GALLERIES, NEW YORK CITY

THE GETTYSBURG ADDRESS (PAGE 116)
NOVEMBER 19, 1863
1987, OIL ON CANVAS
30″ x 30″
MR. AND MRS. HAROLD BERNSTEIN

THE REPULSE (PAGES 100-101)
GETTYSBURG, JULY 3, 1863
1993, MIXED MEDIA
10 3/8″ x 19 1/2″
HAMMER GALLERIES, NEW YORK CITY

A LONG WAY FROM HOME (PAGE 110)
1993, MIXED MEDIA
9 3/8″ x 11″
HAMMER GALLERIES, NEW YORK CITY

THE MAJOR WORKS OF MORT KÜNSTLER ARE
AVAILABLE AS LIMITED EDITION FINE ART PRINTS,
PUBLISHED EXCLUSIVELY BY AMERICAN PRINT
GALLERY, GETTYSBURG, PENNSYLVANIA. CALL
(800) 448-1863 FOR MORE INFORMATION AND THE
ADDRESS OF THE NEAREST AUTHORIZED DEALER.

Roll Call

The number following an individual's name indicates his age at the time of the battle of Gettysburg. The state he called home follows his age. If an officer had close family in two states, both are given.

ALEXANDER, EDWARD PORTER. *28. GEORGIA. WEST POINT, CLASS OF 1857. COLONEL, COMMANDER OF ARTILLERY, LONGSTREET'S CORPS, ARMY OF NORTHERN VIRGINIA. DIRECTED ARTILLERY BARRAGE THAT PRECEDED PICKETT'S CHARGE. DIED APRIL 28, 1910.*

ARCHER, JAMES J. *45. MARYLAND. BRIGADIER GENERAL, COMMANDER OF BRIGADE IN HETH'S DIVISION, A. P. HILL'S CORPS, ARMY OF NORTHERN VIRGINIA. CAPTURED JULY 1, 1863. EXCHANGED AUGUST 1864. DIED OF DISEASE OCTOBER 24, 1864.*

ARMISTEAD, LEWIS A. *46. VIRGINIA. DISMISSED FROM WEST POINT, 1836; JOINED REGULAR ARMY. BRIGADIER GENERAL, COMMANDER OF BRIGADE IN PICKETT'S DIVISION, LONGSTREET'S CORPS, ARMY OF NORTHERN VIRGINIA. MORTALLY WOUNDED IN PICKETT'S CHARGE JULY 3, 1863. DIED JULY 5.*

BARKSDALE, WILLIAM. *41. MISSISSIPPI. POLITICIAN. BRIGADIER GENERAL, COMMANDER OF BRIGADE IN LAFAYETTE MCLAWS'S DIVISION, LONGSTREET'S CORPS, ARMY OF NORTHERN VIRGINIA. MORTALLY WOUNDED JULY 2, 1863. DIED JULY 3.*

BUFORD, JOHN. *37. KENTUCKY, ILLINOIS. WEST POINT, CLASS OF 1848. MAJOR GENERAL, COMMANDER OF CAVALRY DIVISION IN ARMY OF THE POTOMAC, WHICH OPENED THE BATTLE OF GETTYSBURG ON UNION SIDE. DIED OF TYPHOID FEVER DECEMBER 16, 1863.*

CHAMBERLAIN, JOSHUA LAWRENCE. *34. MAINE. GRADUATE OF BOWDOIN COLLEGE, PHI BETA KAPPA, 1852, AND OF BANGOR THEOLOGICAL SEMINARY, 1855. PROFESSOR AT BOWDOIN COLLEGE; ENLISTED IN UNION ARMY 1862. COLONEL OF THE 20TH MAINE INFANTRY AT GETTYSBURG, WHERE HE WON THE CONGRESSIONAL MEDAL OF HONOR FOR THE DEFENSE OF LITTLE ROUND TOP. DIED FEBRUARY 24, 1914.*

CUSTER, GEORGE ARMSTRONG. *23. OHIO. WEST POINT, CLASS OF 1861. BRIGADIER GENERAL, COMMANDER OF CAVALRY BRIGADE, ARMY OF THE POTOMAC. KILLED AT BATTLE OF LITTLE BIG HORN, MONTANA, JUNE 24, 1876.*

DAVIS, JEFFERSON. *55. MISSISSIPPI. WEST POINT, CLASS OF 1828. PRESIDENT, CONFEDERATE STATES OF AMERICA, ELECTED FEBRUARY 9, 1861. CAPTURED BY UNION CAVALRY MAY 10, 1865. DIED DECEMBER 9, 1889.*

DOUBLEDAY, ABNER. *43. NEW YORK. WEST POINT, CLASS OF 1842. BRIGADIER GENERAL, COMMANDER OF DIVISION IN 1ST CORPS, ARMY OF THE POTOMAC. TEMPORARILY SUCCEEDED TO COMMANDER OF CORPS WHEN JOHN REYNOLDS WAS KILLED. DIED JANUARY 26, 1893.*

EARLY, JUBAL A. *46. VIRGINIA. WEST POINT, CLASS OF 1847. MAJOR GENERAL, COMMANDER OF DIVISION IN EWELL'S CORPS, ARMY OF NORTHERN VIRGINIA. DIED MARCH 2, 1894.*

EWELL, RICHARD S. *46. VIRGINIA. WEST POINT, CLASS OF 1840. LIEUTENANT GENERAL, COMMANDER OF CORPS IN ARMY OF NORTHERN VIRGINIA. WOUNDED AND LOST LEG AT SECOND MANASSAS. DIED JANUARY 25, 1872.*

GARNETT, RICHARD B. *45. VIRGINIA. WEST POINT, CLASS OF 1841. BRIGADIER GENERAL, PICKETT'S DIVISION, LONGSTREET'S CORPS, ARMY OF NORTHERN VIRGINIA. EARLIER REMOVED FROM COMMAND OF STONEWALL BRIGADE BY STONEWALL JACKSON FOR ORDERING RETREAT AT BATTLE OF KERNSTOWN. KILLED IN ACTION AT PICKETT'S CHARGE JULY 3, 1863.*

GIBBON, JOHN. *36. NORTH CAROLINA. WEST POINT, CLASS OF 1847. BRIGADIER GENERAL, COMMANDER OF DIVISION IN 2ND CORPS, ARMY OF THE POTOMAC, THAT BORE THE BRUNT OF PICKETT'S CHARGE. WOUNDED IN THE FIGHT. THREE BROTHERS FOUGHT FOR THE CONFEDERACY. DIED FEBRUARY 6, 1896.*

HAMPTON, WADE. *45. SOUTH CAROLINA. GRADUATE OF SOUTH CAROLINA COLLEGE, 1836. REPUTED TO BE WEALTHIEST PLANTER IN SOUTH. BRIGADIER GENERAL, COMMANDER OF CAVALRY BRIGADE IN STUART'S CAVALRY CORPS, ARMY OF NORTHERN VIRGINIA. WOUNDED AT GETTYSBURG. DIED APRIL 11, 1902.*

HANCOCK, WINFIELD SCOTT. *39. PENNSYLVANIA. WEST POINT, CLASS OF 1844. MAJOR GENERAL, COMMANDER OF 2ND CORPS, ARMY OF THE POTOMAC. WOUNDED AT GETTYSBURG. UNSUCCESSFUL CANDIDATE FOR PRESIDENT, 1880. DIED FEBRUARY 9, 1886.*

HETH, HENRY. *37. VIRGINIA. WEST POINT, CLASS OF 1847. MAJOR GENERAL, COMMANDER OF DIVISION IN A. P. HILL'S CORPS, ARMY OF NORTHERN VIRGINIA. WOUNDED AT GETTYSBURG. DIED SEPTEMBER 27, 1899.*

HILL, AMBROSE POWELL. *37. VIRGINIA. WEST POINT, CLASS OF 1847. LIEUTENANT GENERAL, CORPS COMMANDER IN ARMY OF NORTHERN VIRGINIA. KILLED IN ACTION AT PETERSBURG APRIL 2, 1865.*

HOOD, JOHN BELL. *32. KENTUCKY, TEXAS. WEST POINT, CLASS OF 1853. MAJOR GENERAL, COMMANDER OF DIVISION IN LONGSTREET'S CORPS, ARMY OF NORTHERN VIRGINIA. WOUNDED AT GETTYSBURG. DIED AUGUST 30, 1879.*

HOOKER, JOSEPH. *49. MASSACHUSETTS. WEST POINT, CLASS OF 1837. MAJOR GENERAL, COMMANDER OF ARMY OF THE POTOMAC JANUARY 26, 1863–JUNE 28, 1863. RELIEVED OF COMMAND ON THE EVE OF GETTYSBURG. DIED OCTOBER 31, 1879.*

HOWARD, OLIVER O. *32. MAINE. GRADUATE OF BOWDOIN COLLEGE, 1850. WEST POINT, CLASS OF 1854. LOST ARM AT FAIR OAKS. MAJOR GENERAL, COMMANDER OF THE 11TH CORPS, ARMY OF THE POTOMAC. VOTED THE THANKS OF CONGRESS FOR THE DEFENSE OF CEMETERY HILL. DIED OCTOBER 26, 1899.*

JACKSON, THOMAS J. ("STONEWALL"). *AGED 39 AT TIME OF DEATH. VIRGINIA. WEST POINT, CLASS OF 1846. LIEUTENANT GENERAL, CORPS COMMANDER IN ARMY OF NORTHERN VIRGINIA. WOUNDED AT CHANCELLORSVILLE MAY 2, 1863. DIED OF PNEUMONIA MAY 10.*

KEMPER, JAMES L. *40. VIRGINIA. GRADUATE OF WASHINGTON COLLEGE, 1842. LAWYER AND POLITICIAN. BRIGADIER GENERAL, COMMANDED BRIGADE IN PICKETT'S DIVISION, LONGSTREET'S CORPS, ARMY OF NORTHERN VIRGINIA. WOUNDED AND CAPTURED IN PICKETT'S CHARGE. EXCHANGED 1864. DIED APRIL 7, 1895.*

LEE, ROBERT E. *56. VIRGINIA. WEST POINT, CLASS OF 1829. APPOINTED COMMANDER OF ARMY OF NORTHERN VIRGINIA JUNE 1, 1862 AND GENERAL IN CHIEF OF CONFEDERATE ARMIES JANUARY 31, 1865. DIED OCTOBER 22, 1870.*

LINCOLN, ABRAHAM. *54. ILLINOIS. PRESIDENT, UNITED STATES, ELECTED NOVEMBER 6, 1860, REELECTED NOVEMBER 8, 1864. CALLED OUT TROOPS TO SUPPRESS INSURRECTION APRIL 15, 1861. DELIVERED GETTYSBURG ADDRESS NOVEMBER 19, 1863. MORTALLY WOUNDED BY ASSASSIN APRIL 14, 1865. DIED APRIL 15.*

LONGSTREET, JAMES. *42. SOUTH CAROLINA, ALABAMA. WEST POINT, CLASS OF 1842. LIEUTENANT GENERAL, CORPS COMMANDER IN ARMY OF NORTHERN VIRGINIA. DIED JANUARY 2, 1904.*

MEADE, GEORGE GORDON. *47. PENNSYLVANIA. WEST POINT, CLASS OF 1845. MAJOR GENERAL, APPOINTED COMMANDER OF ARMY OF THE POTOMAC JUNE 28, 1863. DIED NOVEMBER 6, 1872.*

PETTIGREW, JAMES JOHNSTON. *34. NORTH CAROLINA. GRADUATE OF UNIVERSITY OF NORTH CAROLINA, 1847. LAWYER. BRIGADIER GENERAL, HETH'S DIVISION, A. P. HILL'S CORPS, ARMY OF NORTHERN VIRGINIA. ASSUMED COMMAND OF DIVISION WHEN HETH WAS WOUNDED; LED IT IN PICKETT'S CHARGE. LIGHTLY WOUNDED JULY 3, 1863; MORTALLY WOUNDED IN RETREAT FROM GETTYSBURG JULY 14, 1863. DIED JULY 17.*

PICKETT, GEORGE E. *38. VIRGINIA. WEST POINT, CLASS OF 1846. MAJOR GENERAL, COMMANDER OF DIVISION IN LONGSTREET'S CORPS, ARMY OF NORTHERN VIRGINIA. DIED JULY 30, 1875.*

REYNOLDS, JOHN F. *42. PENNSYLVANIA. WEST POINT, CLASS OF 1841. MAJOR GENERAL, COMMANDER OF 1ST CORPS, ARMY OF THE POTOMAC. KILLED IN ACTION AT GETTYSBURG JULY 1, 1863.*

SICKLES, DANIEL E. *43. NEW YORK. LAWYER AND POLITICIAN. MAJOR GENERAL, COMMANDER OF 3RD CORPS, ARMY OF THE POTOMAC. LOST LEG AT GETTYSBURG. DIED MAY 3, 1914.*

STEPHENS, ALEXANDER H. *51. GEORGIA. VICE PRESIDENT, CONFEDERATE STATES OF AMERICA, ELECTED FEBRUARY 9, 1861. DIED MARCH 4, 1883.*

STUART, JAMES EWELL BROWN ("JEB"). *30. VIRGINIA. WEST POINT, CLASS OF 1854. MAJOR GENERAL, COMMANDER OF CAVALRY CORPS, ARMY OF NORTHERN VIRGINIA. MORTALLY WOUNDED MAY 11, 1864, AT BATTLE OF YELLOW TAVERN. DIED MAY 12.*

TRIMBLE, ISAAC R. *61. MARYLAND. WEST POINT, CLASS OF 1822. WOUNDED AT SECOND MANASSAS; REJOINED ARMY OF NORTHERN VIRGINIA JUST BEFORE GETTYSBURG. BRIGADIER GENERAL, GIVEN COMMAND OF WILLIAM D. PENDER'S DIVISION (PENDER WAS MORTALLY WOUNDED JULY 2, 1862), A. P. HILL'S CORPS, WHICH HE LED IN PICKETT'S CHARGE. WOUNDED AND CAPTURED JULY 3, 1863; LOST LEG. EXCHANGED FEBRUARY 1865. DIED JANUARY 2, 1888.*

Chronology

1860

NOVEMBER 6	SLAVE STATES CALL CONVENTIONS TO CONSIDER SECESSION, FOLLOWING ABRAHAM LINCOLN'S ELECTION AS THE FIRST ANTISLAVERY PRESIDENT
DECEMBER 20	SOUTH CAROLINA IS THE FIRST OF SEVEN STATES TO SECEDE IN THE NEXT SIX WEEKS

1861

FEBRUARY 4	CONVENTION OF SECEDED STATES IN MONTGOMERY, ALABAMA
FEBRUARY 8	CONSTITUTION OF CONFEDERATE STATES OF AMERICA (CSA) ADOPTED
FEBRUARY 9	CSA ELECTS JEFFERSON DAVIS PROVISIONAL PRESIDENT
FEBRUARY 18	INAUGURATION OF JEFFERSON DAVIS
MARCH 4	INAUGURATION OF ABRAHAM LINCOLN AS PRESIDENT OF THE UNITED STATES
APRIL 8	U.S. FLEET DEPARTS NEW YORK TO RESUPPLY FORT SUMTER, SOUTH CAROLINA
APRIL 12	CONFEDERATES ATTACK FORT SUMTER
APRIL 13	FORT SUMTER SURRENDERS
APRIL 15	LINCOLN CALLS OUT MILITIA TO SUPPRESS INSURRECTION
APRIL 17	VIRGINIA IS THE FIRST OF FOUR MORE SLAVE STATES TO SECEDE
JULY 21	FIRST BATTLE OF BULL RUN (MANASSAS)

1862

FEBRUARY 6	UNION CAPTURE OF FORT HENRY, TENNESSEE
FEBRUARY 16	UNION CAPTURE OF FORT DONELSON, TENNESSEE
FEBRUARY 22	JEFFERSON DAVIS INAUGURATED PRESIDENT OF THE CONFEDERACY FOR SIX-YEAR TERM
FEBRUARY 25	NASHVILLE IS FIRST CONFEDERATE STATE CAPITAL TO FALL TO UNION FORCES
APRIL 6-7	BATTLE OF SHILOH
APRIL 16	CONFEDERATES ENACT CONSCRIPTION
APRIL 25	NEW ORLEANS FALLS TO UNION NAVY
JUNE 1	ROBERT E. LEE TAKES COMMAND OF THE ARMY OF NORTHERN VIRGINIA AFTER JOSEPH E. JOHNSTON IS WOUNDED IN BATTLE OF SEVEN PINES
JUNE 25–JULY 1	SEVEN DAYS BATTLES DRIVE THE UNION FORCES AWAY FROM RICHMOND
AUGUST 29-30	SECOND BATTLE OF BULL RUN (MANASSAS)
SEPTEMBER 4	ARMY OF NORTHERN VIRGINIA CROSSES POTOMAC RIVER TO INVADE MARYLAND
SEPTEMBER 17	BATTLE OF ANTIETAM
SEPTEMBER 22	LINCOLN ISSUES PRELIMINARY EMANCIPATION PROCLAMATION
DECEMBER 13	BATTLE OF FREDERICKSBURG

1863

JANUARY 1	LINCOLN ISSUES FINAL EMANCIPATION PROCLAMATION
MARCH 3	UNION GOVERNMENT ENACTS CONSCRIPTION
MAY 1-6	BATTLE OF CHANCELLORSVILLE
MAY 10	STONEWALL JACKSON DIES OF PNEUMONIA FOLLOWING AMPUTATION OF HIS ARM AT CHANCELLORSVILLE
MAY 15	CONFEDERATE GOVERNMENT APPROVES LEE'S PLAN TO INVADE PENNSYLVANIA
JUNE 6	LEE'S ARMY BEGINS TO MOVE NORTH
JUNE 16	FIRST CONFEDERATE UNITS CROSS THE POTOMAC
JUNE 25	JEB STUART'S CAVALRY BEGINS RAID IN REAR OF UNION ARMY
JUNE 28	GEORGE G. MEADE REPLACES JOSEPH HOOKER AS COMMANDER OF THE ARMY OF THE POTOMAC
JUNE 30	JOHN BUFORD'S UNION CAVALRY ENTERS GETTYSBURG
JULY 1, EARLY MORNING	ADVANCE UNITS OF HENRY HETH'S INFANTRY DIVISION OF THE ARMY OF NORTHERN VIRGINIA CLASH WITH BUFORD'S CAVALRY

JULY 1, MIDMORNING	JOHN REYNOLDS'S 1ST CORPS OF THE ARMY OF THE POTOMAC ARRIVES; STOPS CONFEDERATE ADVANCE; REYNOLDS KILLED
JULY 1, EARLY AFTERNOON	CONFEDERATES RENEW ATTACK; EWELL'S CORPS ARRIVES AND ATTACKS UNION 11TH CORPS; LEE ARRIVES ON BATTLEFIELD
JULY 1, LATE AFTERNOON	UNION LINE BREAKS; SURVIVORS RETREAT THROUGH TOWN TO CEMETERY HILL
	LEE GIVES EWELL DISCRETIONARY ORDERS TO ATTACK CEMETERY HILL; EWELL DOES NOT ATTACK
JULY 1, MIDNIGHT	MEADE ARRIVES ON BATTLEFIELD; DECIDES TO STAY AND FIGHT
JULY 2, MORNING	LONGSTREET RECOMMENDS MANEUVER TO SOUTH; LEE DISAGREES AND ORDERS LONGSTREET TO ATTACK UNION LEFT ON CEMETERY RIDGE
JULY 2, 4:00 P.M. TO DARK	LONGSTREET'S ATTACK; HEAVY FIGHTING IN PEACH ORCHARD, WHEAT FIELD, DEVIL'S DEN, LITTLE ROUND TOP, CEMETERY RIDGE
JULY 2, DUSK	UNITS OF EWELL'S CORPS ATTACK CEMETERY AND CULP'S HILLS WITH LIMITED SUCCESS; STUART'S CAVALRY AND GEORGE PICKETT'S INFANTRY DIVISION ARRIVE ON BATTLEFIELD
JULY 2, MIDNIGHT	AFTER COUNSEL WITH SUBORDINATES, MEADE DECIDES TO STAY AND FIGHT
JULY 3, MORNING	UNION 12TH CORPS ATTACKS AND RETAKES TRENCHES ON CULP'S HILL
JULY 3, AFTERNOON	CAVALRY BATTLE THREE MILES EAST OF GETTYSBURG BLOCKS STUART'S ADVANCE TOWARD UNION REAR
JULY 3, 1:07 P.M.	CONFEDERATE ARTILLERY BARRAGE BEGINS, PRECEDING PICKETT'S ASSAULT
JULY 3, 3:00–4:00 P.M.	ATTACK ON UNION CENTER, SPEARHEADED BY PICKETT'S DIVISION; REPULSED, WITH HEAVY CONFEDERATE LOSS
JULY 4	CONFEDERATES BEGIN RETREAT TO VIRGINIA
	VICKSBURG SURRENDERS TO ULYSSES S. GRANT'S ARMY
JULY 13–16	NEW YORK CITY DRAFT RIOTS
JULY 14	CONFEDERATES RECROSS POTOMAC TO VIRGINIA
JULY 18	UNION ASSAULT ON FORT WAGNER, SOUTH CAROLINA, SPEARHEADED BY 54TH MASSACHUSETTS INFANTRY; REPULSED, WITH HEAVY LOSS; BLACK SOLDIERS PRAISED
SEPTEMBER 19–20	BATTLE OF CHICKAMAUGA
NOVEMBER 19	LINCOLN'S GETTYSBURG ADDRESS
NOVEMBER 23–25	BATTLES OF CHATTANOOGA OPEN UNION GATEWAY TO GEORGIA

1864

MAY 5–JUNE 18	CAMPAIGN FROM WILDERNESS TO PETERSBURG, VIRGINIA; SIEGE OF PETERSBURG BEGINS
MAY 7–SEPTEMBER 2	SHERMAN'S ATLANTA CAMPAIGN, CULMINATING IN SURRENDER OF ATLANTA
NOVEMBER 15–DECEMBER 20	SHERMAN'S MARCH FROM ATLANTA TO THE SEA
NOVEMBER 30	BATTLE OF FRANKLIN
DECEMBER 15–16	BATTLE OF NASHVILLE DESTROYS CONFEDERATE ARMY OF TENNESSEE

1865

FEBRUARY 1–MARCH 23	SHERMAN'S MARCH THROUGH THE CAROLINAS
APRIL 2	FALL OF RICHMOND AND PETERSBURG
APRIL 9	LEE SURRENDERS AT APPOMATTOX
APRIL 14	ASSASSINATION OF LINCOLN
JUNE 23	LAST CONFEDERATE ARMY SURRENDERS
DECEMBER 18	THIRTEENTH AMENDMENT TO CONSTITUTION RATIFIED, ABOLISHING SLAVERY

Suggested Reading

Catton, Bruce. *Gettysburg: The Final Fury*. New York: Berkeley Books, 1974.

———. *Glory Road: The Bloody Route from Fredericksburg to Gettysburg*. Garden City, N.Y.: Doubleday, 1952.

Clark, Champ, and editors of Time-Life Books. *Gettysburg: The Confederate High Tide*. Alexandria, Va.: Time-Life Books, 1985.

Cleaves, Freeman. *Meade of Gettysburg*. Dayton, Ohio: Morningside Bookshop, 1980.

Coddington, Edwin B. *The Gettysburg Campaign: A Study in Command*. New York: Scribner's, 1968.

Connelly, Thomas L. *The Marble Man: Robert E. Lee and His Image in American Society*. New York: Knopf, 1977.

Dowdey, Clifford. *Death of a Nation: The Story of Lee and His Men at Gettysburg*. New York: Knopf, 1958.

Foote, Shelby. *The Civil War: A Narrative*. 3 vols. New York: Random House, 1958–74.

Frassanito, William A. *Gettysburg: A Journey in Time*. New York: Scribner's, 1975.

Freeman, Douglas Southall. *R. E. Lee: A Biography*. 4 vols. New York: Scribner's, 1934–35. One-volume abridgement, 1961.

———. *Lee's Lieutenants: A Study in Command*. 3 vols. New York: Scribner's, 1944.

Gallagher, Gary, ed. *The First Day at Gettysburg*. Kent, Ohio: Kent State University Press, 1992.

Hassler, William W. *Crisis at the Crossroads: The First Day at Gettysburg*. Tuscaloosa: University of Alabama Press, 1970.

Hergeden, Lance, and William J. K. Beaudot. *In the Bloody Railroad Cut at Gettysburg*. Dayton, Ohio: Morningside Bookshop, 1990.

McPherson, James M., ed. *Battle Chronicles of the Civil War*. 6 vols. New York: Macmillan, 1989.

———. *Battle Cry of Freedom: The Civil War Era*. New York: Oxford University Press, 1988.

Moe, Richard. *The Last Full Measure: The Life and Death of the First Minnesota Volunteers*. New York: Holt, 1993.

Nolan, Alan T. *The Iron Brigade: A Military History*. New York: Macmillan, 1961.

———. *Lee Considered: General Robert E. Lee and Civil War History*. Chapel Hill: University of North Carolina Press, 1991.

Pfanz, Harry. *Gettysburg—The Second Day*. Chapel Hill: University of North Carolina Press, 1987.

Piston, William Garrett. *Lee's Tarnished Lieutenant: James Longstreet and His Place in Southern History*. Athens: University of Georgia Press, 1987.

Pullen, John J. *The Twentieth Maine*. Dayton, Ohio: Morningside Bookshop, 1983.

Stewart, George R. *Pickett's Charge*. Dayton, Ohio: Morningside Bookshop, 1983.

Thomas, Emory M. *Bold Dragoon: The Life of J.E.B. Stewart*. New York: Harper & Row, 1986.

———. *The Confederate Nation: 1861–1865*. New York: Harper & Row, 1979.

Trulock, Alice Rains. *In the Hands of Providence: Joshua L. Chamberlain and the American Civil War*. Chapel Hill: University of North Carolina Press, 1992.

Tucker, Glenn. *High Tide at Gettysburg: The Campaign in Pennsylvania*. Indianapolis: Bobbs-Merrill, 1958.

———. *Lee and Longstreet at Gettysburg*. Indianapolis: Bobbs-Merrill, 1968.

Wills, Gary. *Lincoln at Gettysburg: The Words That Remade America*. New York: Simon & Schuster, 1992.

Index

Photo Credits

- PAGE 36—U. S. ARTILLERY OFFICER'S HAT. COURTESY KENNESAW MOUNTAIN MILITARY ANTIQUES AND JACK W. MELTON, JR. PHOTO BY J. STOLL.

- PAGE 38—CONFEDERATE OFFICER'S SWORD. COURTESY STEVE AND PATRICIA MULLINAX COLLECTION. PHOTO BY J. STOLL.

- PAGE 42—U. S. FLAG. COURTESY HOWARD MADAUS COLLECTION. PHOTO BY LUCILLE WARTERS.

- PAGE 43—CONFEDERATE DRUM. COURTESY STEVE AND PATRICIA MULLINAX COLLECTION. PHOTO BY J. STOLL.

- PAGE 52—U. S. MODEL 1858 CANTEEN. COURTESY KENNESAW MOUNTAIN MILITARY ANTIQUES AND JACK W. MELTON, JR. PHOTO BY J. STOLL.

- PAGE 53—U. S. MODEL 1851 OFFICER'S SWORD BELT PLATE. COURTESY WALTER AND CYNDI TIMOSCHUK COLLECTION. PHOTO BY J. STOLL.

- PAGE 63—KING WILLIAM LIGHT ARTILLERY, ARMY OF NORTHERN VIRGINIA, BATTLE FLAG WITH BATTLE HONORS. COURTESY THE MUSEUM OF THE CONFEDERACY, RICHMOND, VIRGINIA. PHOTO BY KATHERINE WETZEL.

- PAGE 69—SADDLE BELONGING TO GENERAL LEE. COURTESY THE MUSEUM OF THE CONFEDERACY, RICHMOND, VIRGINIA. PHOTO BY KATHERINE WETZEL.

- PAGE 74—CONFEDERATE CARTRIDGE BOX. COURTESY STEVE AND PATRICIA MULLINAX COLLECTION. PHOTO BY J. STOLL.

- PAGE 77—CONFEDERATE WOODEN DRUM CANTEEN. COURTESY STEVE AND PATRICIA MULLINAX COLLECTION. PHOTO BY J. STOLL.

- PAGE 84—FAYETTEVILLE RIFLE WITH BAYONET. PRIVATE COLLECTION. PHOTO BY J. STOLL.

- PAGE 92—SPILLER & BURR REVOLVER. COURTESY STEVE AND PATRICIA MULLINAX COLLECTION. PHOTO BY J. STOLL.

- PAGE 94—CIVIL WAR ARTILLERY SHELLS. COURTESY CHRISTOPHER L. TARAS COLLECTION. PHOTO BY J. STOLL.

- PAGE 97—U. S. BOX PLATE WITH LODGED, CONFEDERATE STATES, ENFIELD .58 CALIBER BULLET. COURTESY STONE MOUNTAIN RELICS, STONE MOUNTAIN, GEORGIA. PHOTO BY J. STOLL.

- PAGE 98—CIVIL WAR BULLETS. COURTESY KENNESAW MOUNTAIN MILITARY ANTIQUES AND JACK W. MELTON, JR. PHOTO BY J. STOLL.

- PAGE 125—POCKET WATCH (CIRCA 1850) WITH LODGED .58 CALIBER THREE-RINGER (U. S.) BULLET. COURTESY OF STONE MOUNTAIN RELICS, STONE MOUNTAIN, GEORGIA. PHOTO BY J. STOLL.

- PAGE 127—BULLETS CARVED BY CIVIL WAR SOLDIERS. COURTESY STONE MOUNTAIN RELICS, STONE MOUNTAIN, GEORGIA. PHOTO BY J. STOLL.

- PAGE 128—CONFEDERATE BUGLE MADE OF BRASS AND TIN. COURTESY STEVE AND PATRICIA MULLINAX COLLECTION. PHOTO BY J. STOLL.